Stimmt!

AQA GCSE German
Higher
Vocabulary Book

Published by Pearson Education Limited, 80 Strand, London, WC2R 0RL
www.pearsonschoolsandfecolleges.co.uk
Text © Pearson Education Limited 2017
Editorial management by Gwladys Rushworth for Haremi
Edited by Anne Urbschat
Typeset by York Publishing Solutions Pvt. Ltd.
Cover image: Getty Images: PhotoDisc / Kathrin Ziegler
Cover © Pearson Education Limited 2017

Written by Melissa Weir

First published 2023
10

British Library Cataloguing in Publication Data
A catalogue record for this book is available from the British Library.
ISBN 978 1 292 13240 2

Copyright notice
All rights reserved. No part of this publication may be reproduced in any form or by any means (including photocopying or storing it in any medium by electronic means and whether or not transiently or incidentally to some other use of this publication) without the written permission of the copyright owner, except in accordance with the provisions of the Copyright, Design and Patents Act 1988 or under the terms of a license issued by the Copyright Licensing Agency, Barnard's Inn, 86 Fetter Lane, London EC4A 1EN (www.cla.co.uk). Applications for the copyright owner's written permission should be addressed to the publisher.

Printed by Bell and Bain Ltd, Glasgow

High-frequency words

verpassen	to miss
versprechen	to promise
verzeihen	to forgive
weinen	to cry
wissen	to know
wünschen	to wish

Had a look ☐ **Nearly there** ☐ **Nailed it** ☐

anrufen	to phone
antworten	to answer
beantworten	to answer
beschreiben	to describe
besprechen	to discuss
sich bewerben um	to apply for
denken	to think
diskutieren	to discuss
erklären	to explain
erzählen	to tell
fragen	to ask
informieren	to inform
mitteilen	to inform
plaudern	to chat
reden	to talk
sagen	to say
schreiben	to write
sprechen	to speak
eine Frage stellen	to ask a question
telefonieren (mit)	to phone
tippen	to type
unterschreiben	to sign
wiederholen	to repeat
zuhören	to listen

Had a look ☐ **Nearly there** ☐ **Nailed it** ☐

annehmen	to accept
bekommen	to receive
beschließen	to decide
bevorzugen	to prefer
brauchen	to need
sich entscheiden	to decide
erhalten	to receive
erlauben	to allow
erwarten	to expect
fehlen	to be missing
sich freuen auf	to look forward to
gefallen	to please
gern haben	to like
hassen	to hate
sich interessieren für	to be interested in
verhindern	to prevent
vermeiden	to avoid
vorhaben	to intend
werden	to become

Had a look ☐ **Nearly there** ☐ **Nailed it** ☐

anfangen	to begin
aufhören	to stop
beenden	to end
beginnen	to begin
dauern	to last
enden	to finish, to end
erreichen	to reach
geschehen	to happen
gewinnen	to win
nachsehen	to check
notieren	to note
organisieren	to organise
passieren	to happen
planen	to plan
produzieren	to produce
scheitern	to fail
schiefgehen	to go wrong
verbessern	to improve
verlieren	to lose
versuchen	to try
vorstellen	to introduce

Had a look ☐ **Nearly there** ☐ **Nailed it** ☐

bedienen	to serve
befehlen	to order (command)
benutzen	to use
beraten	to advise
bestellen	to order (food)
bitten um	to ask for
danken	to thank
empfehlen	to recommend
füllen	to fill
geben	to give
gelingen	to succeed
raten	to advise
reparieren	to repair
reservieren	to reserve
retten	to save, to rescue
schicken	to send
wechseln	to change

Had a look ☐ **Nearly there** ☐ **Nailed it** ☐

finden	to find
glauben	to believe, to think
haben	to have
heißen	to be called
hoffen	to hope
hören	to hear
kennen	to know (be familiar with)
nennen	to name
schauen	to look
scheinen	to seem, to shine
sehen	to see
verstehen	to understand
wählen	to choose, to dial

5

High-frequency words

zeigen	to show
dürfen	to be allowed to
können	to be able to
mögen	to like
müssen	to have to
sollen	to be supposed to
wollen	to want
zusehen	to look, to watch

Had a look ☐ **Nearly there** ☐ **Nailed it** ☐

ausgeben	to spend (money)
einkaufen	to shop
einschalten	to light, to turn on
kaufen	to buy
klicken	to click
klingeln	to ring
kosten	to cost
leihen	to borrow, to hire
mieten	to rent, to hire
schneien	to snow
schweigen	to be silent
stehlen	to steal
verdienen	to earn
verkaufen	to sell
zahlen	to pay
zählen	to count

Had a look ☐ **Nearly there** ☐ **Nailed it** ☐

Common adjectives

ärgerlich	annoying
böse	angry
dumm	stupid
eilig	in a hurry
ermüdend	tiring
ernst	serious
erschöpft	exhausted
faul	lazy
launisch	moody
laut	loud, noisy
müde	tired
schüchtern	shy
schwach	weak
schwer	heavy, serious
streng	strict
traurig	sad
zornig	angry

Had a look ☐ **Nearly there** ☐ **Nailed it** ☐

artig	well-behaved
brav	well-behaved
beschäftigt	busy
dankbar	grateful
dynamisch	dynamic
fleißig	hard-working

geduldig	patient
gesund	healthy
glücklich	happy
gut gelaunt	in a good mood
komisch	funny, comical
lustig	funny
nett	kind, nice
reif	mature, ripe
reizend	charming
schnell	fast, quick
stark	strong
stolz	proud
verantwortlich	responsible
zufrieden	satisfied

Had a look ☐ **Nearly there** ☐ **Nailed it** ☐

groß	big, tall
klein	little, small
lang	long
kurz	short
hoch	high
niedrig	low
breit	broad
schmal	slim, narrow
dicht	dense
eng	narrow, tight
dünn	thin
rund	round
steil	steep
nah	near
weit	far
voll	full
leer	empty
erst–	first
letzt–	last
nächst–	next

Had a look ☐ **Nearly there** ☐ **Nailed it** ☐

alt	old
jung	young
jünger	younger
dick	fat
schlank	slim
hübsch	pretty
schön	beautiful
hässlich	ugly
krank	ill
reich	rich
satt	full

Had a look ☐ **Nearly there** ☐ **Nailed it** ☐

gut	good
ausgezeichnet	excellent
fantastisch	fantastic

High-frequency words

großartig	magnificent	typisch	typical
klasse	sensational	unterschiedlich	variable
perfekt	perfect	wertvoll	valuable
prima	marvellous	wichtig	important
toll	great	wirklich	real(ly)
wunderbar	wonderful	zahlreich	numerous
Lieblings-	favourite		
aufregend	exciting		
spannend	exciting, tense		

Had a look ☐ **Nearly there** ☐ **Nailed it** ☐

ekelhaft	disgusting
enttäuscht	disappointed
langweilig	boring
schlecht	bad
schrecklich	awful, terrible

Had a look ☐ **Nearly there** ☐ **Nailed it** ☐

		alle	all
		eigen	own
		ander-	other
		einzig	only
		allein	alone
		zusammen	together
		leise	quiet
		lautlos	soundless, silent
bequem	comfortable	friedlich	peaceful
dreckig	dirty	ruhig	calm
flexibel	flexible	frei	free, vacant
gebrochen	broken	bereit	ready
gefährlich	dangerous	fertig	ready
geöffnet	open	leicht	easy, light
geschlossen	closed	schwierig	difficult
heiß	hot	schwer	hard, heavy, difficult
kaputt	broken	erstaunlich	astonishing
kostenlos	free (of charge)	unglaublich	unbelievable
neu	new	unvorstellbar	unimaginable
nötig	necessary	erfreut	pleased
notwendig	necessary	erstaunt	astonished
offen	open	überrascht	surprised
sauber	clean		
schmutzig	dirty		

Had a look ☐ **Nearly there** ☐ **Nailed it** ☐

teuer	expensive
umweltfeindlich	environmentally damaging
umweltfreundlich	environmentally friendly
weich	soft
zerbrochen	broken

Common adverbs

oben	above, upstairs
unten	below, downstairs
vorwärts	forwards
rückwärts	backwards
hier	here
da	there
dort	there
da drüben	over there
irgendwo	somewhere
draußen	outside
mitten (in / auf / an / …)	in the middle of
unterwegs	en route, on the way
immer	always
oft	often
regelmäßig	regularly
manchmal	sometimes
kaum	barely, hardly
nie	never
neulich	recently
sofort	immediately, straight away

Had a look ☐ **Nearly there** ☐ **Nailed it** ☐

allgemein	general
bestimmt	definite
echt	real(ly)
wahr	true
richtig	correct, right
falsch	false
aktuell	current
ehemalig	old, former
genau	exact
gleich	same
gültig	valid
klar	clear
möglich	possible
nützlich	useful

Had a look ☐ **Nearly there** ☐ **Nailed it** ☐

7

High-frequency words

besonders	especially
sehr	very
wirklich	really
ziemlich	rather, quite
zu	too
immer noch	still
fast	almost
genug	enough
jedoch	however
leider	unfortunately
vielleicht	perhaps
wahrscheinlich	probably
besser	better
gern	willingly
lieber	rather (preferably)
mehr	more
nur	only
schon	already
langsam	slowly
schnell	quickly

Had a look ☐ **Nearly there** ☐ **Nailed it** ☐

Prepositions

bis	until
durch	through
entlang	along
für	for
gegen	against
ohne	without
um	around
wider	against

Had a look ☐ **Nearly there** ☐ **Nailed it** ☐

aus	out of
außer	except
bei	at, with, next to
gegenüber	opposite
mit	with
nach	after
seit	since
von	from
zu	to
hin zu	towards

Had a look ☐ **Nearly there** ☐ **Nailed it** ☐

an	at
auf	on
hinter	behind
in	in, into
neben	next to
über	above, over
unter	beneath, under

vor	in front of
zwischen	between

Had a look ☐ **Nearly there** ☐ **Nailed it** ☐

statt	instead of
trotz	despite
während	during
wegen	because of

Had a look ☐ **Nearly there** ☐ **Nailed it** ☐

Colours

die Farbe	colour
blau	blue
braun	brown
dunkel	dark
gelb	yellow
grau	grey
grün	green
hell	light
lila	violet
rosa	pink
rot	red
schwarz	black
weiß	white

Had a look ☐ **Nearly there** ☐ **Nailed it** ☐

Numbers

eins	one (1)
zwei	two (2)
drei	three (3)
vier	four (4)
fünf	five (5)
sechs	six (6)
sieben	seven (7)
acht	eight (8)
neun	nine (9)
zehn	ten (10)
elf	eleven (11)
zwölf	twelve (12)
dreizehn	thirteen (13)
vierzehn	fourteen (14)
fünfzehn	fifteen (15)
sechzehn	sixteen (16)
siebzehn	seventeen (17)
achtzehn	eighteen (18)
neunzehn	nineteen (19)
zwanzig	twenty (20)

Had a look ☐ **Nearly there** ☐ **Nailed it** ☐

einundzwanzig	twenty-one (21)
zweiundzwanzig	twenty-two (22)

High-frequency words

dreiundzwanzig	twenty-three (23)
vierundzwanzig	twenty-four (24)
fünfundzwanzig	twenty-five (25)
sechsundzwanzig	twenty-six (26)
siebenundzwanzig	twenty-seven (27)
achtundzwanzig	twenty-eight (28)
neunundzwanzig	twenty-nine (29)
dreißig	thirty (30)

Had a look ☐ **Nearly there** ☐ **Nailed it** ☐

vierzig	forty (40)
fünfzig	fifty (50)
sechzig	sixty (60)
siebzig	seventy (70)
achtzig	eighty (80)
neunzig	ninety (90)
hundert	(one) hundred (100)
einhundert	(one) hundred (100)
hunderteins	one hundred and one (101)
hundertzwanzig	one hundred and twenty (120)
zweihundert	two hundred (200)
tausend	one thousand (1,000)
eintausend	one thousand (1,000)
tausendeinhundert	one thousand one hundred (1,100)
elfhundert	one thousand one hundred (1,100)
zweitausend	two thousand (2,000)
(eine) Million	one million (1,000,000)
zwei Millionen	two million (2,000,000)

Had a look ☐ **Nearly there** ☐ **Nailed it** ☐

erster/erste/erstes	first
zweiter/zweite/zweites	second
elfter/elfte/elftes	eleventh
einundzwanzigster/ einundzwanzigste/ einundzwanzigstes	twenty-first

Had a look ☐ **Nearly there** ☐ **Nailed it** ☐

Quantities and measures

viele	many
mehrere	several
genug	enough
ein bisschen	a little
ein Drittel	a third (of)
ein Dutzend	a dozen
eine Dose	a tin (of)
eine Flasche	a bottle (of)
ein Glas	a jar (of)
eine Kiste	a box (of)
eine Packung	a packet (of)
eine Schachtel	a box (of)
eine Scheibe	a slice (of)
ein Stück	a piece (of)
eine Tafel	a bar (of)
eine Tüte	a bag (of)

Had a look ☐ **Nearly there** ☐ **Nailed it** ☐

Some useful connecting words

aber	but
also	so
anstatt	instead
auch	also
außerdem	additionally, moreover
dafür	instead
danach	afterwards
dann	then
deshalb	for this reason
deswegen	for this reason
jedoch	however
nachher	afterwards, later
oder	or
übrigens	by the way, moreover
und	and
vorher	beforehand
weil	because
zuerst	first of all

Had a look ☐ **Nearly there** ☐ **Nailed it** ☐

Time expressions

der Tag(e)	day
der Morgen(–)	morning
der Vormittag(e)	morning
der Nachmittag(e)	afternoon
der Abend(e)	evening
die Nacht (Nächte)	night
Mitternacht	midnight
die Woche(n)	week
das Wochenende(n)	weekend
gestern	yesterday
heute	today
morgen	tomorrow
morgen früh	tomorrow morning
übermorgen	the day after tomorrow
vorgestern	the day before yesterday
die Minute(n)	minute

Had a look ☐ **Nearly there** ☐ **Nailed it** ☐

ab	from
ab und zu	now and then
von Zeit zu Zeit	from time to time
am Anfang	at the start
bald	soon

High-frequency words

früh	early
heutzutage	nowadays
immer	always
immer noch	still
jetzt	now
meistens	mostly
nächst–	next
pünktlich	on time
rechtzeitig	on time
seit	since
sofort	immediately
spät	late
später	later
täglich	every day, daily
wöchentlich	weekly

Had a look ☐ **Nearly there** ☐ **Nailed it** ☐

Times of day

(um) ein Uhr	(at) one o'clock
13.00 Uhr	one o'clock (1 p.m.)
dreizehn Uhr	one o'clock (1 p.m.)
21.00 Uhr	nine o'clock (9 p.m.)
einundzwanzig Uhr	nine o'clock (9 p.m.)
neun Uhr abends	nine o'clock in the evening
genau um 14.00 Uhr	at exactly two o'clock (2 p.m.)
genau um vierzehn Uhr	at exactly two o'clock (2 p.m.)
gegen … Uhr	at about … o'clock
ungefähr um … Uhr	at about … o'clock
es ist 3.05 Uhr	it is five past three
es ist drei Uhr fünf	it is five past three
fünf vor drei	five to three
zehn nach vier	ten past four
zehn vor vier	ten to four
Viertel vor sechs	quarter to six
Viertel nach sieben	quarter past seven
halb elf	half past ten

Had a look ☐ **Nearly there** ☐ **Nailed it** ☐

Days of the week

Montag	Monday
Dienstag	Tuesday
Mittwoch	Wednesday
Donnerstag	Thursday
Freitag	Friday
Samstag	Saturday
Sonnabend	Saturday
Sonntag	Sunday
(am) Montag	(on) Monday
(am) Montagvormittag	(on) Monday morning
(am) Montagabend	(on) Monday evening
montags	on Mondays
jeden Montag	every Monday

Had a look ☐ **Nearly there** ☐ **Nailed it** ☐

Months and seasons

der Monat(e)	month
Januar	January
Februar	February
März	March
April	April
Mai	May
Juni	June
Juli	July
August	August
September	September
Oktober	October
November	November
Dezember	December
die Jahreszeit(en)	season
(im) Frühling	(in) spring
(im) Sommer	(in) summer
(im) Herbst	(in) autumn
(im) Winter	(in) winter

Had a look ☐ **Nearly there** ☐ **Nailed it** ☐

Question words

wann?	when?
warum?	why?
was für?	what sort of?
was?	what?
wen? wem?	whom?
wer?	who?, whom?
wessen?	whose?
wie viel(e)?	how much?, how many?
wie?	how?
wo?	where?

Had a look ☐ **Nearly there** ☐ **Nailed it** ☐

Other useful expressions

Es gibt …	There is/are …
Hier gibt es …	Here is/are …
Man darf nicht …	You are not allowed to …
Man muss …	You/one must …
Wie schreibt man das?	How do you spell that?
Was bedeutet das?	What does that mean?
Noch einmal?	Once again?
Ich verstehe nicht.	I don't understand.
Ich weiß es nicht.	I don't know.
Es geht mir gut.	I'm fine.
Ich bin satt.	I'm full. / I've had enough (to eat).
Natürlich!	Of course!
In Ordnung!	OK! (in agreement)
Mit Vergnügen!	With pleasure!
Viel Glück!	Good luck!
Schade!	Too bad! / What a shame!
Genug davon!	That's enough!

Had a look ☐ **Nearly there** ☐ **Nailed it** ☐

High-frequency words

Opinions

Meiner Meinung nach …	*In my opinion …*
Ich denke, dass …	*In my opinion …*
Persönlich …	*Personally, …*
Das interessiert mich nicht.	*That doesn't interest me / appeal to me.*
Es ärgert mich.	*It annoys me.*
Es bringt mich zum Lachen.	*It makes me laugh.*
Es gefällt mir.	*I like it.*
Es ist mir egal.	*I don't mind.*
Es kommt darauf an.	*It depends.*
Es lohnt sich nicht.	*It's not worth it.*
Es macht nichts.	*It doesn't matter.*

Had a look ☐ Nearly there ☐ Nailed it ☐

Other useful words

ja	*yes*
nein	*no*
das	*that*
etwas	*something*
ob	*whether, if*
wenn	*if, when*
wie	*as, like*
alle	*everyone*
jeder	*everybody*
jemand	*someone*
zum Beispiel	*for example*

Had a look ☐ Nearly there ☐ Nailed it ☐

das Ding(e)	*thing*
die Sache(n)	*thing*
der Gegenstand (-stände)	*object*
die Form(en)	*shape*
die Art(en)	*type*
die Weise(n)	*way*
die Nummer(n)	*number*
das Mal(e)	*time*
die Zahl(en)	*figure, number*
die Mitte(n)	*middle*
das Ende(n)	*end*
Herr …	*Mr …*
Frau …	*Mrs …*

Had a look ☐ Nearly there ☐ Nailed it ☐

Countries

Belgien	*Belgium*
Dänemark	*Denmark*
Deutschland	*Germany*
England	*England*
Frankreich	*France*
Griechenland	*Greece*
Großbritannien	*Great Britain*
Indien	*India*
Irland	*Ireland*
Italien	*Italy*
die Niederlande	*the Netherlands*
Österreich	*Austria*
Polen	*Poland*
Russland	*Russia*
die Schweiz	*Switzerland*
Schottland	*Scotland*
Spanien	*Spain*
die Türkei	*Turkey*
die USA	*the United States*
die Vereinigten Staaten	*the United States*
Wales	*Wales*

Had a look ☐ Nearly there ☐ Nailed it ☐

Continents

Afrika	*Africa*
Asien	*Asia*
Australien	*Australia*
Europa	*Europe*
Nordamerika	*North America*
Südamerika	*South America*

Had a look ☐ Nearly there ☐ Nailed it ☐

Nationalities

Amerikaner(in)	*American*
amerikanisch	*American*
Belgier(in)	*Belgian*
belgisch	*Belgian*
Brite/Britin	*British*
britisch	*British*
Däne/Dänin	*Danish*
dänisch	*Danish*
Deutsche(r)	*German*
deutsch	*German*
Engländer(in)	*English*
englisch	*English*
Franzose/Französin	*French*
französisch	*French*
Grieche/Griechin	*Greek*
griechisch	*Greek*
Inder(in)	*Indian*
indisch	*Indian*
Ire/Irin	*Irish*
irisch	*Irish*

Had a look ☐ Nearly there ☐ Nailed it ☐

Italiener(in)	*Italian*
italienisch	*Italian*
Niederländer(in)	*Dutch*
niederländisch	*Dutch*
Österreicher(in)	*Austrian*
österreichisch	*Austrian*

High-frequency words

Pakistani	Pakistani
pakistanisch	Pakistani
Russe/Russin	Russian
russisch	Russian
Schotte/Schottin	Scottish
schottisch	Scottish
Schweizer(in)	Swiss
schweizerisch	Swiss
Spanier(in)	Spanish
spanisch	Spanish
Türke/Türkin	Turkish
türkisch	Turkish
Waliser(in)	Welsh
walisisch	Welsh

Had a look ☐ Nearly there ☐ Nailed it ☐

Places

Bayern	Bavaria
Köln	Cologne
München	Munich
Wien	Vienna
die Alpen	the Alps
der Schwarzwald	the Black Forest
die Donau	the Danube
der Rhein	the Rhine
der Bodensee	Lake Constance
der Ärmelkanal	the English Channel
der Eurotunnel	the Channel Tunnel

Had a look ☐ Nearly there ☐ Nailed it ☐

Social conventions

Guten Tag!	Good day!
Guten Abend!	Good evening!
Gute Nacht!	Good night!
Grüß Gott!	Hello!
Auf Wiedersehen!	Goodbye!
Bis später!	See you later!
Bis bald!	See you soon!
Bis morgen!	See you tomorrow!
Entschuldigung!	Excuse me!
Hilfe!	Help!
Wie bitte?	I beg your pardon?
Alles Gute!	All the best!
Mit bestem Gruß	Best wishes
bitte	please
danke schön	thank you very much
Bitte schön!	You're welcome!

Had a look ☐ Nearly there ☐ Nailed it ☐

Language used in dialogues and messages

Rufen Sie mich an!	Call me! (formal)
Ruf mich an!	Call me! (informal)
Kann ich etwas ausrichten?	Can I take a message?
Ich verbinde Sie.	I will put you through.
Ich höre zu.	I'm listening.
Ich bin gleich wieder da.	I'll be right back.
Warten Sie einen Moment.	Wait a moment.
Betreff ...	Regarding ...
In Bezug auf ...	Further to / Following ...
Zu Händen von ...	For the attention of ...

Had a look ☐ Nearly there ☐ Nailed it ☐

das Telefon(e)	telephone
der Hörer(-)	receiver (telephone)
der Ton (Töne)	tone
die Vorwahl(en)	area code
die Telefonnummer wählen	to dial the number
im Gespräch mit	in communication with
am Apparat	on the line / speaking
der Augenblick(e)	moment
für jetzt	for the moment
falsche Nummer	wrong number
die SMS(-)	text message
simsen	to text
die E-Mail(s)	email
gesandt von	sent by
eigentlich	in fact

Had a look ☐ Nearly there ☐ Nailed it ☐

Kapitel 1 Wörter

Words I should know for speaking and writing activities

Schulfächer / School subjects

Sprachen	languages
Deutsch	German
Englisch	English
Französisch	French
Spanisch	Spanish
Naturwissenschaft(en)	science(s)
Biologie	biology
Chemie	chemistry
Physik	physics
Mathe(matik)	math(ematic)s
Informatik	ICT
Geschichte	history
Erdkunde	geography
Politik	politics
Gesellschaft	sociology
Wirtschaft	economics
Kunst	art
Musik	music
Theater	drama
Religion	RE
Sport	PE, sport
das Wahlfach	optional subject
das Pflichtfach	compulsory subject

Had a look ☐ Nearly there ☐ Nailed it ☐

Kleidung / Clothes

Ich trage (nie) ...	I (never) wear ...
einen Rock	a skirt
eine Jeans	jeans
eine Hose	trousers
eine Jacke	a jacket
eine Krawatte	a tie
ein Hemd	a shirt
ein Kleid	a dress
ein T-Shirt	a T-shirt
Sportschuhe	trainers
Schuhe	shoes

Had a look ☐ Nearly there ☐ Nailed it ☐

Schulsachen / School items

Was hast du (für das neue Schuljahr / die neunte Klasse) gekauft?	What have you bought (for the new school year / Year 9)?
Ich habe ... gekauft.	I bought ...
einen Bleistift	a pencil
einen Füller	a fountain pen
einen Kuli	a ballpoint pen
einen Radiergummi	a rubber
einen Taschenrechner	a calculator
ein Etui	a pencil case
ein Lineal	a ruler
Filzstifte	felt-tip pens

Had a look ☐ Nearly there ☐ Nailed it ☐

Das neue Schuljahr / The new school year

In der neunten Klasse freue ich mich (nicht) auf ...	I'm (not) looking forward to ... in Year 9.
den Druck	the pressure
die Klassenfahrt	the class trip
das Zeugnis	the report
die Hausaufgaben	the homework
die (Sport-)AG(s)	the sport club(s)
die Klassenarbeiten	the tests
die Prüfungen	the exams
neue Fächer	new subjects
meine Freunde/Freundinnen	my friends
die Noten	the grades
am meisten	mostly
total	totally
(echt) sehr	(really) very
weniger	less
(gar) nicht	not (at all)
nie	never
langweilig	boring
stressig	stressful
schwierig	difficult
interessant	interesting
einfach	simple

Had a look ☐ Nearly there ☐ Nailed it ☐

Ein Schultag / A school day

Was hat (die Klasse 9) in der (ersten) Stunde am (Montag)?	What does (Year 9) have in the (first) lesson on (Monday)?
zweite(n)	second
dritte(n)	third
vierte(n)	fourth
fünfte(n)	fifth
sechste(n)	sixth
siebte(n)	seventh
Die Schule beginnt um ...	School starts at ...
Die Schule endet um ...	School ends at ...
die (kleine) Pause	(short) break
die Mittagspause	lunch break
Wir haben ... Stunden pro Tag.	We have ... lessons per day.
Jede Stunde dauert ... Minuten.	Each lesson lasts ... minutes.

13

Kapitel 1 Wörter

Ich habe vier Stunden pro Woche (Erdkunde).	I have four lessons of (geography) per week.	immer Hochdeutsch sprechen	always speak standard German
Ich habe viermal pro Woche (Mathe).	I have (maths) four times a week.	ruhig sein	be quiet
Mein Lieblingsfach ist (Physik).	My favourite subject is (physics).	höflich sein	be polite
		pünktlich sein	be punctual
		respektvoll sein	be respectful

Had a look ☐ **Nearly there** ☐ **Nailed it** ☐   **Had a look** ☐ **Nearly there** ☐ **Nailed it** ☐

Fragen stellen — Asking questions

Wann?	When?
Wie viele?	How many?
Um wie viel Uhr?	At what time?
Wie oft?	How often?
Was?	What?
Ist (Mathe) dein Lieblingsfach?	Is (maths) your favourite subject?
Warum?	Why?
Welches Fach?	Which subject?
Wie?	How?
Wer?	Who?

zu	too
sehr	very
ziemlich	rather, quite
streng	strict
ärgerlich	annoying
nervig	irritating
(un)gerecht	(un)just
(un)fair	(un)fair
locker	casual, informal

Had a look ☐ **Nearly there** ☐ **Nailed it** ☐   **Had a look** ☐ **Nearly there** ☐ **Nailed it** ☐

Die Schulordnung — School rules

der Computerraum	ICT room
der Schulhof	playground
die Aula	assembly hall
die Bibliothek	library
die Kantine	canteen
die Sporthalle	sports hall
das Klassenzimmer	classroom
das Labor	lab(oratory)
das Lehrerzimmer	staff room
die Toiletten	toilets

Das deutsche Schulsystem — The German school system

Ich besuche …	I go to …
die Grundschule	primary school
die Gesamtschule	comprehensive school
die Hauptschule	a type of secondary modern school
die Realschule	a type of secondary modern school
das Gymnasium	grammar school
die Oberstufe	sixth form
die Ganztagsschule	all-day school
das Internat	boarding school
der Mittlere Schulabschluss	German equivalent of GCSEs
das Abitur	German equivalent of A levels

Had a look ☐ **Nearly there** ☐ **Nailed it** ☐

Wir dürfen nicht …	We are not allowed to …
Wir dürfen weder … noch …	We are allowed neither … nor …
schlagen	to hit
mobben	to bully
(auf dem Schulgelände) rauchen	to smoke (in the school grounds)
essen	to eat
trinken	to drink
Sportschuhe tragen	wear trainers
Handball spielen	play handball
Wir dürfen keine Schimpfwörter sagen.	We are not allowed to use swear words.
Wir dürfen keinen Kaugummi kauen.	We are not allowed to chew gum.
Wir müssen … den Müll trennen	We have to … separate the rubbish

gemischt	mixed
privat	private
staatlich	state
Man hat …	We have …
(k)einen Stundenplan	no / a timetable
(k)eine Schuluniform	no / a school uniform
(keine) Hausaufgaben	(no) homework
Man hat tolle / keine Computerräume.	We have great / no ICT rooms.
Die Schule ist prima ausgestattet.	The school is very well equipped.
Die Schule ist schlecht ausgestattet.	The school is very well badly equipped.
Ich bin sitzen geblieben.	I repeated the year.
Ich muss das Jahr wiederholen.	I have to repeat the year.

Had a look ☐ **Nearly there** ☐ **Nailed it** ☐

Eine Klassenfahrt / *A class trip*

Was werden wir am (Mittwoch) machen?	What will we do on (Wednesday)?
Ich werde …	I will …
Deutsch sprechen	speak German
einen Schultag erleben	experience a school day
einen Tagesausflug machen	go on a day trip
eine Fahrradtour machen	go on a cycling tour
ein Kunstprojekt machen	do an art project
den Abend bei einer Gastfamilie verbringen	spend the evening with a host family
das (Zirkus-)Museum besuchen	visit the (circus) museum
den Freizeitpark besuchen	visit the theme park
die Sehenswürdigkeiten besichtigen	visit the sights
ins Hallenbad / Freibad gehen	go to the indoor / outdoor swimming pool
in der Altstadt bummeln	stroll around the old town
Andenken kaufen	buy souvenirs
(wieder) nach Hause fahren	go home (again)
Es wird … kosten.	It will cost …
Das wird Spaß machen.	That will be fun.
Heimweh haben	to be homesick
reisekrank sein	to be travel sick
Die Reise hat … gedauert.	The journey lasted …
Das war eine Katastrophe!	That was a catastrophe!
Es gab (kein) WLAN.	There was (no) Wi-Fi.

Had a look ☐ **Nearly there** ☐ **Nailed it** ☐

Extra words I should know for reading and listening activities

Schularbeit / School work

die Durchschnittsnote	average grade
ausgezeichnet	excellent
befriedigend	fair
ausreichend	satisfactory
mangelhaft	poor
ungenügend	unsatisfactory
stark	strong, good at (subject)
schwach	weak, bad at (subject)
begabt	gifted
aufpassen	to pay attention
üben	to practise
verbessern	to improve
(eine Prüfung) bestehen*	to pass (an exam)
die Leistung(en)	achievement
die Strafarbeit(en)	written punishment, lines
die Geisteswissenschaften	humanities (subjects)
die Zeitverschwendung	waste of time
das Trimester(–)	term
die Zukunft	future

Had a look ☐ Nearly there ☐ Nailed it ☐

In der Schule / At school

die Tafel	board (e.g. whiteboard)
das Sprachlabor	language lab
die Rezeption	reception
der Sportplatz(–plätze)	sports field
der Anschluss	connection (e.g. internet)
das Netzwerk(e)	network
die Renovierung(en)	renovation
die Erlaubnis	permission

Had a look ☐ Nearly there ☐ Nailed it ☐

Auf Austausch / On an exchange

der Austausch	exchange
der Ausweis	identity card
das Erlebnis(se)	experience
die Gegend(en)	area, region
die Grenze(n)	border
der Reisepass	passport
die Abschiedsparty(s)	farewell party
die Willkommensparty(s)	welcome party
eine Reise wert sein	to be worth a trip
Angst vor … haben	to be afraid / scared of …
besuchen	to visit
sich melden bei	to get in touch with
mitbringen**	to bring (with you)
mitmachen**	to join in, to take part in
stattfinden	to take place
übernachten	to stay, to spend the night
überqueren	to cross
wandern	to go hiking

Had a look ☐ Nearly there ☐ Nailed it ☐

---

*Watch out for false friends! To say 'to pass an exam' in German, you don't use *passieren* (which means 'to happen'). Instead, you need the verb *bestehen*:

Ich hoffe, ich werde meine Prüfungen bestehen.
I hope I will pass my exams.

Note that *bestehen* is irregular in the perfect tense:

Ich habe meine Prüfungen bestanden.
I passed my exams.

**Break unfamiliar verbs down into their component parts to work out their meaning:

mitmachen: mit + machen → to join in, to take part (literally: to do (something) with)

mitbringen: mit + bringen → to bring with (you)

mitnehmen: mit + nehmen → to take with (you)

Kapitel 2 Wörter

Words I should know for speaking and writing activities

Freizeitaktivitäten — Leisure activities

die Freizeit	leisure time, free time
Briefmarken sammeln	to collect stamps
Plüschtiere sammeln	to collect soft toys
Sport machen	to do sport
Sport treiben	to do sport
Fußball spielen	to play football
Hockey spielen	to play hockey
Basketball spielen	to play basketball
Schach spielen	to play chess
Karten spielen	to play cards
am Computer spielen	to play on the computer
Computerspiele spielen	to play computer games
im Internet surfen	to surf on the internet
im Internet chatten	to chat on the internet
mit Freunden reden	to chat with friends
mit Freunden chillen	to chill with friends
Freunde treffen	to meet friends
Zeit mit dem besten Freund/der besten Freundin verbringen	to spend time with your best friend
ins Kino gehen	to go to the cinema
in die Stadt gehen	to go into town
abends fernsehen	to watch TV in the evening
am Wochenende Videos gucken	to watch videos at the weekend
Filme sehen	to watch films
die Nachrichten sehen	to watch the news

Had a look ☐   Nearly there ☐   Nailed it ☐

Musik machen	to make music
Radio hören	to listen to the radio
Bücher lesen	to read books
faulenzen	to chill, to laze about
nichts tun	to do nothing
Ich bin …	I am …
(nicht) sehr	(not) very
ziemlich	quite
ein bisschen	a bit
(gar) nicht	not (at all)
sportlich	sporty
musikalisch	musical
faul	lazy
abenteuerlustig	adventurous

Had a look ☐   Nearly there ☐   Nailed it ☐

Instrumente — Instruments

die Blockflöte	recorder
die Flöte	flute
die Geige	violin
die (elektrische) Gitarre	(electric) guitar
die Klarinette	clarinet
die Trompete	trumpet
das Keyboard	keyboard
das Klavier	piano
das Saxofon	saxophone
das Schlagzeug	drums
Ich spiele kein Instrument.	I don't play an instrument.

Had a look ☐   Nearly there ☐   Nailed it ☐

Bücher — Books

gedruckt	printed
das Buch (Bücher)	book
das gedruckte Buch	printed book
die Biografie(n)	biography
der Comic(s)	comic book
der Fantasyroman(e)	fantasy novel
die Horrorgeschichte(n)	horror story
die Komödie(n)	comedy
der Krimi(s)	detective / crime story
die Liebesgeschichte(n)	love story
das Science-Fiction-Buch (–Bücher)	sci-fi-book
der Thriller(–)	thriller

Had a look ☐   Nearly there ☐   Nailed it ☐

die Zeitung(en)	newspaper
die Zeitschrift(en)	magazine
das Magazin(e)	magazine
die Illustrierte(n)	(glossy) magazine
das Blog(s)	blog
das E-Book(s)	e-book
das Taschenbuch (–bücher)	paperback book
Ich lese (oft / nie) Taschenbücher …	I (often / never) read paperbacks …
auf meinem Tablet / E-Reader	on my tablet / e-reader
auf einem elektronischen Gerät	on an electronic device
im Bett	in bed
in meinem Zimmer	in my room
im Bus	on the bus
der Akku	rechargeable battery
der Bildschirm	screen

Had a look ☐   Nearly there ☐   Nailed it ☐

Musik — Music

Ich interessiere mich für viele Musikrichtungen.	I'm interested in lots of types of music.
die Musiksammlung	music collection
Ich höre (nicht) gern …	I (don't) like listening to …
Ich höre lieber …	I prefer to listen to …

Kapitel 2 Wörter

Ich höre am liebsten …	I like listening to … best of all.	die Gameshow(s)	game show
klassische Musik	classical music	die Realityshow(s)	reality show
Opernmusik	opera	die Dokumentation(en)	documentary
Popmusik	pop music	die Nachrichten (pl)	the news
Reggae	reggae	Ich finde (Serien) blöd).	I find (series) (silly).
R&B-Musik	R&B	Ich habe (die Sendung / den Film) (großartig) gefunden.	I found (the programme / film) (great).
Rapmusik	rap		
Heavy Metal-Musik	heavy metal		
Country-und-Western-Musik	country and western	**Had a look** ☐ **Nearly there** ☐ **Nailed it** ☐	
Jazzmusik	jazz	Die Sendung / Der Film / Die Handlung war …	The programme / film / plot, story line was …
Livemusik	live music	Die Schauspieler waren …	The actors were …

Had a look ☐ **Nearly there** ☐ **Nailed it** ☐

Ich höre Musik auf meinem …	I listen to music on my …	(un)realistisch	(un)realistic
Handy / Smartphone	mobile phone / smartphone	schwach	weak
		enttäuschend	disappointing
		überzeugend	convincing
		humorvoll	humorous, amusing
Laptop / Tablet	laptop / tablet	(Der Film) macht keinen Sinn.	(The film) doesn't make sense.
Musik herunterladen / downloaden	to download music	Ich bin von (der Sendung / dem Film) (nicht) begeistert, weil …	I'm (not) enthusiastic about (the programme / film) because …
Das ist praktisch.	That's practical.		
Ich spiele seit (einem Jahr) Gitarre.	I have been playing guitar for (a year).		
Ich downloade alles auf mein Tablet.	I download everything onto my tablet.	Ich empfehle (die Sendung / den Film), weil …	I recommend (the programme / film) because …
Das spart so viel Platz.	That saves so much space.		
Der Ton (auf einem Tablet) ist nicht gut.	The sound (on a tablet) is not good.	**Had a look** ☐ **Nearly there** ☐ **Nailed it** ☐	
Die Qualität ist fantastisch.	The quality is fantastic.	**Sport**	**Sport**
Die Eintrittskarten sind zu teuer.	The entry tickets are too expensive.	Ski fahren	to go skiing
		snowboarden	to go snowboarding
Ich gebe kein Geld für (Musik) aus.	I don't spend any money on (music).	rodeln	to sledge, to toboggan
		eislaufen	to ice skate
Das ist ein tolles Gefühl.	That's a great feeling.	Curling spielen	to do curling

Had a look ☐ **Nearly there** ☐ **Nailed it** ☐

		Nordic Walking machen	to go Nordic walking
		wandern	to hike
Film und Fernsehen	**Film and television**	klettern	to climb
der Film(e)	film, movie	schwimmen	to swim
der Actionfilm(e)	action movie	Fahrrad / Rad fahren	to cycle
der Fantasyfilm(e)	fantasy film	Handball spielen	to play handball
der Horrorfilm(e)	horror film	Fußball spielen	to play football
die Komödie(n)	comedy	Tennis spielen	to play tennis

Had a look ☐ **Nearly there** ☐ **Nailed it** ☐

der Krimi(s)	detective / crime film		
der Liebesfilm(e)	romance	Ich spiele gern (Fußball).	I like playing (football).
der Science-Fiction-Film(e)	sci-fi film	Ich turne seit (fünf Jahren).	I have been doing gymnastics for (five years).
der Thriller(–)	thriller	Ich mache (nicht) gern (Nordic Walking).	I (don't) like doing (Nordic walking).
der Zeichentrickfilm(e)	cartoon		
Ich sehe gern fern.	I like watching TV.	Ich habe mit (sechs) Jahren angefangen, Tennis zu spielen.	I started to play tennis when I was (six) years old.
der Zuschauer(–)	viewer		
das Fernsehen	television		
die Fernsehsendung(en)	TV programme		
die Serie(n)	series		

Kapitel 2 Wörter

Ich habe (Rollschuhlaufen) im Alter von (sechs) Jahren gelernt.	I learned to (roller skate) at the age of (six).	Es gibt … Reden / Feste / Konzerte	There is/are … speeches / celebrations / concerts
Ich habe schon (Golf) ausprobiert.	I have already tried (golf).	Musik / Tanz / tolle Kostüme	music / dancing / great costumes
Ich würde (nie) (Skateboard fahren).	I would (never) do (skateboarding).	Proteste / ein Feuerwerk	protests / fireworks
Ich trainiere (jeden Tag) mit Freunden im Verein.	I train with friends at the club (every day).	Ich bin (auf den Weihnachtsmarkt) gegangen.	I went (to the Christmas market).
die Bodenübung	floor work	Das war der Höhepunkt des Jahres.	That was the highlight of the year.
der Hochweitsprung	high long jump	Die Stimmung war super.	The atmosphere was great.
der 100-Meter-Lauf	100-metre sprint	Ich habe (Lebkuchen) gegessen / gekauft.	I ate / bought (gingerbread).
das Ringen	wrestling		
das Schwingen	another type of wrestling	Am Ende des Tages war ich (völlig satt / müde).	At the end of the day I was (totally full / tired).
das Steinheben	stone lifting		
das Steinstoßen	stone tossing	Ich würde gern (auf einen Markt in England) gehen.	I would like to go (to a market in England).
der Weitsprung	long jump		

Had a look ☐ **Nearly there** ☐ **Nailed it** ☐

Es würde mich interessieren, … zu sehen.	I would be interested in seeing …
Ich könnte über … lernen.	I could learn about …
Ich werde nächstes Jahr (in England) feiern.	Next year I will celebrate (in England).

Feste und Feiertage — Festivals and celebrations

am 24. Dezember (usw.)	on the 24th December (etc.)
feiern	to celebrate
(Zeit) verbringen	to spend (time)
stattfinden	to take place
zu Ostern	at Easter
zu Weihnachten	at Christmas
der Feiertag(e)	public holiday
der Festzug(-züge)	procession
der Karneval	carnival
der Fasching	carnival
der Maibaum(-bäume)	may pole
die Fete(n)	party
das Fest(e)	festival, fair
das Feuerwerk(e)	fireworks (pl)
das Geschenk(e)	present
das Volksfest(e)	(traditional) fair

Had a look ☐ **Nearly there** ☐ **Nailed it** ☐

Had a look ☐ **Nearly there** ☐ **Nailed it** ☐

K2

19

Kapitel 2 Wörter

Extra words I should know for reading and listening activities

Freizeit — *Leisure time*

das Brettspiel	board game
die Festplatte	hard drive
der Fotoapparat	camera
die Freizeitbeschäftigung	leisure activity
die Kopfhörer (pl)	headphones
der Lautsprecher (–)	(loud)speaker
der Rhythmus	rhythm
die Spielkonsole	games console
die Unterhaltung	entertainment
das Vinyl	vinyl (records)
die Volksmusik	folk music
bequem	comfortable
entspannend	relaxing
griffbereit	handy
kostenlos	free (of charge)
gratis	free (of charge)
lebhaft	lively
unhandlich	unwieldy
verändern	to change
stundenlang	for hours

Had a look ☐ Nearly there ☐ Nailed it ☐

Film und Fernsehen — *Film and television*

die Atmosphäre	atmosphere
die Fernbedienung(en)	remote control
die Kurzfassung(en)	summary
die Originalfassung(en)	original version
das Satellitenfernsehen	satellite TV
die Spezialeffekte (pl)	special effects
die Szene	scene
das Thema	theme, topic
glaubhaft	credible
hervorragend	excellent
humoristisch	humorous
komisch	funny, strange
satirisch	satirical

Had a look ☐ Nearly there ☐ Nailed it ☐

Sport — *Sport*

die Sportart	(type of) sport
der Extremsport	extreme sport
das Bergsteigen	mountaineering
das Fallschirmspringen	parachuting
das Fechten	fencing
der Federball	badminton
die Leichtathletik	(field and track) athletics
das Radrennen	cycle racing
das Rudern	rowing
das Turnier	tournament
der Wettkampf	competition
der Gegner	opponent
die Ausdauer	stamina, endurance
die Kraft	strength
die Schnelligkeit	speed
die Eisbahn	ice rink
die Kletterwand	climbing wall
der Teamgeist	team spirit
ausprobieren	to try (out)
überholen	to overtake
werfen	to throw
gefährlich	dangerous

Had a look ☐ Nearly there ☐ Nailed it ☐

Feste und Feiertage — *Celebrations and holidays*

der Arbeitstag	working day
Karfreitag	Good Friday
Ostermontag	Easter Monday
der Osterhase	Easter bunny
das Osterei	Easter egg
die Wiedervereinigung*	reunification
die Vorweihnachtszeit	pre-Christmas period
Heiligabend	Christmas Eve
der Weihnachtsbaum	Christmas tree
der Imbiss	snack
die Wollmütze	woolly hat
das Spielzeug	toy
das Kaufhaus	department store
das Angebot	offer
bieten	to offer
Geld ausgeben	to spend money
genießen	to enjoy
gesetzlich	statutory
die Ruhe	peace, rest

Had a look ☐ Nearly there ☐ Nailed it ☐

⭐ *Don't be daunted by long, tricky-looking words. Look carefully at the words they are made up of and try to work out the meaning based on the words you know.*

die Wiedervereinigung

You know that *wieder* means 'again' and *der Verein* is 'club' (i.e. somewhere where people come together), so *die Wiedervereinigung* is literally 'the coming together again', or 'reunification'.

Man feiert die Wiedervereinigung Deutschlands am 3. Oktober. We celebrate the reunification of Germany on 3 October.

Kapitel 3 Wörter

Words I should know for speaking and writing activities

Charaktereigenschaften | *Personal characteristics*

Er/Sie ist ... | *He/She is ...*
abenteuerlustig | *adventurous*
aktiv | *active*
cool | *cool*
dynamisch | *dynamic*
fleißig | *hard-working*
frech | *cheeky*
freundlich | *friendly*
intelligent | *intelligent*
kreativ | *creative*
langweilig | *boring*
locker | *laid-back*
lustig | *funny*
modisch | *fashionable*
nett | *nice*
originell | *original*
selbstbewusst | *self-confident*
sportlich | *sporty*
unterhaltsam | *entertaining*

Had a look ☐ **Nearly there** ☐ **Nailed it** ☐

Aussehen | *Appearance*

Sie hat (braune) Haare. | *She has (brown) hair.*
blond | *blonde*
braun | *brown*
grau | *grey*
schwarz | *black*
rotbraun | *auburn*
kurz | *short*
lang | *long*
glatt | *straight*
dunkel | *dark*
hell | *light*
Er/Sie hat (blaue) Augen. | *He/She has (blue) eyes.*
Er/Sie trägt ... | *He/She wears ...*
eine Brille | *glasses*
eine Sonnenbrille | *sunglasses*
Er hat einen Bart. | *He has a beard.*
Sie hat Sommersprossen. | *She has freckles.*
Er/Sie ist ... | *He/She is ...*
hübsch | *pretty*
schlank | *slim*

Had a look ☐ **Nearly there** ☐ **Nailed it** ☐

Wie ist ein guter Freund/eine gute Freundin? | *What makes a good friend?*

Ein guter Freund/Eine gute Freundin ... | *A good friend ...*
hat immer Zeit für mich | *always has time for me*
ist sympathisch | *is nice*
unterstützt mich immer | *always supports me*
muss hilfsbereit sein | *must be helpful*
muss ehrlich sein | *must be honest*
darf nie auf andere Freunde eifersüchtig sein | *may never be jealous of other friends*
muss viel Geduld haben | *must have lots of patience*
kann mit mir über alles reden | *can talk to me about everything*
hat die gleichen Interessen | *has the same interests*
sieht gut aus | *looks good*
Das ist für mich ... | *That is ... to me.*
(nicht) wichtig | *(not) important*
wichtiger | *more important*
am wichtigsten | *the most important*
Wir sind miteinander befreundet, weil ... | *We are friends with each other because ...*
wir die gleichen Interessen haben | *we have the same interests*
wir viel zusammen lachen | *we laugh a lot together*
wir über alles reden können | *we can talk about everything*
Wir haben uns (in der Grundschule) kennengelernt. | *We met at primary school.*
Wir sind seit (dem Sommer) ein Pärchen. | *We have been a couple since (the summer).*

Had a look ☐ **Nearly there** ☐ **Nailed it** ☐

Beziehungen | *Relationships*

Ich komme (nicht so) gut mit ... aus. | *I (don't) get on (so) well with ...*
Ich verstehe mich (nicht so gut) mit ... | *I (don't) get on (so) well with ...*
Ich kann ihn/sie nicht leiden! | *I can't stand him/her!*
Er/Sie geht mir auf die Nerven. | *He/She gets on my nerves.*
Unsere Beziehung ist (nicht so) gut, weil er/sie ... | *Our relationship is (not so) good ... because he/she is ...*
toll / sympathisch / lieb | *great / nice / kind*
hilfsbereit / ehrlich / ärgerlich ist | *helpful / honest / annoying*
(zu) vorsichtig ist | *(too) careful*
nicht hilfsbereit ist | *not helpful*
weil er/sie (viel / keine) Geduld hat | *because he/she has (a lot of / no) patience*
weil er/sie (immer / nie) Zeit für mich hat | *because he/she (always / never) has time for me*

K 3

21

Kapitel 3 Wörter

weil er/sie mich (nicht) unterstützt	because he/she supports me / doesn't support me

Had a look ☐ Nearly there ☐ Nailed it ☐

Ich streite mich mit …	I argue with …
meinem Vater / ihm	my father / him
meiner Mutter / ihr	my mother / her
meinen Geschwistern / ihnen	my brothers and sisters / them
Wir streiten uns um …	We argue about …
den Computer	the computer
die Kleidung	clothes
das Handy	the mobile phone
Geld	money
Freunde	friends
Wir haben uns um … gestritten.	We argued about …
Er/Sie findet, …	He/She thinks …
Sie finden, …	They think …
ich verbringe zu viel Zeit mit dem Handy	I spend too much time on my mobile
ich verbringe zu viel Zeit am Computer	I spend too much time on the computer
ich mache nicht genug Hausaufgaben	I don't do enough homework
ich gebe zu viel Geld aus	I spend too much money
ich bin eifersüchtig auf (meinen Bruder / meine Schwester)	I'm jealous of (my brother / my sister)
Er/Sie mag meine Kleidung nicht.	He/She doesn't like my clothes.
Sie mögen meine Freunde nicht.	They don't like my friends.

Had a look ☐ Nearly there ☐ Nailed it ☐

Meine perfekte Hochzeit
My perfect wedding

die Blumen (pl)	flowers
die Braut (Bräute)	bride
der Bräutigam(e)	bridegroom
der Trauzeuge(n)	best man
die Brautjungfer(n)	bridesmaid
das Brautkleid(er)	wedding dress
der Ehering(e)	wedding ring
die Einladung(en)	invitation
die Flitterwochen (pl)	honeymoon
der Fotograf(en)	photographer
der Gast (Gäste)	guest
das Hochzeitsauto(s)	wedding car
der Hochzeitstag(e)	wedding day, wedding anniversary
die Hochzeitstorte(n)	wedding cake
die Kirche(n)	church
die Location	venue
der Termin(e)	(wedding) date
die Tischrede(n)	speech
der Verlobte(n)	fiancé
die Verlobte(n)	fiancée
die zivile Partnerschaft(en)	civil partnership

Had a look ☐ Nearly there ☐ Nailed it ☐

abholen	to collect
anschaffen	to buy, to get
ausdrucken	to print out
aussuchen	to choose
auswählen	to select
einladen	to invite
einstellen	to take on, to appoint
festlegen	to set (a date)
stattfinden	to take place
teilnehmen	to take part
vorbereiten	to prepare
Für mich ist die Ehe (nicht) sehr wichtig.	Marriage is (not) very important to me.
Ich finde eine Hochzeit …	I find a wedding …
wirklich romantisch	really romantic
altmodisch	old-fashioned
unglaublich teuer	unbelievably expensive
eine große Geldverschwendung	a big waste of money

Had a look ☐ Nearly there ☐ Nailed it ☐

Mein Wochenende
My weekend

Ich werde am Sonntag / am Wochenende …	On Sunday / At the weekend I will …
Rad fahren	go cycling
spazieren gehen	go for a walk
ins Freibad gehen	go to the open-air pool
im Internet surfen	surf the internet
soziale Netzwerke nutzen	use social networks
Hausaufgaben machen	do homework
in die Kirche gehen	go to church
einkaufen gehen	go shopping
Zeit mit Familie / Freunden verbringen	spend time with family / friends
grillen	have a barbecue
Musik hören	listen to music
einen Film gucken	watch a film
fernsehen	watch TV
bestimmt	definitely
wahrscheinlich	probably
vielleicht	perhaps
nicht	not

Had a look ☐ Nearly there ☐ Nailed it ☐

Kapitel 3 Wörter

Damals und heute / *Then and now*

Als ich ein Kind war, ...	*When I was a child ...*
Mit (zehn) Jahren ...	*At age (ten) ...*
Früher ...	*Before ...*
war das Leben ziemlich schwer	*life was quite hard*
war meine Mutter oft krank	*my mother was often ill*
musste ich immer zu Hause helfen	*I always had to help at home*
konnte ich nie Zeit mit Freunden verbringen	*I could never spend time with my friends*
durfte ich niemanden nach Hause einladen	*I was never allowed to invite anybody to my house*
durfte ich nicht alleine (zur Schule) gehen	*I was not allowed to go (to school) on my own*
konnte ich abends schwimmen	*I could swim in the evenings*
Das war so unfair!	*That was so unfair!*

Had a look ☐ **Nearly there** ☐ **Nailed it** ☐

Heutzutage muss ich viel weniger machen.	*Nowadays I have to do a lot less.*
Im Moment ist es besser.	*At the moment it's better.*
Ich darf mit meinen Freunden ...	*I'm allowed to ... with my friends.*
Ich muss um 21 Uhr nach Hause kommen.	*I have to be home by 9 p.m.*
Das ist ...	*That is ...*
zu früh	*too early*
ein bisschen zu viel	*a bit too much*
Ich will länger ausgehen.	*I want to stay out later.*
Ich habe keine Zeit mehr für ...	*I no longer have any time for ...*
Ich will eine bessere Balance finden.	*I want to find a better balance.*
Ich muss ...	*I must ...*
fleißig in der Schule lernen	*study hard at school*
gute Noten bekommen	*get good grades*
Ich habe viel Freiheit.	*I have a lot of freedom.*
Ich darf ...	*I am allowed to ...*
abends ausgehen	*go out in the evenings*
mein Handy so viel benutzen, wie ich will	*use my mobile as much as I want*
soziale Netzwerke nutzen	*use social networks*
Ich bin doch kein Kind mehr!	*After all, I'm not a child any more!*

Had a look ☐ **Nearly there** ☐ **Nailed it** ☐

Kapitel 3 Wörter

Extra words I should know for reading and listening activities

Positive Charaktereigenschaften	*Positive personal characteristics*
gesund	healthy
gesprächig	chatty
großzügig	generous
klug	clever
lebendig	lively
optimistisch	optimistic
schüchtern	shy
treu	faithful
unabhängig	independent
vernünftig	reasonable
verständnisvoll	understanding
zuverlässig	reliable
guter Laune sein	to be in a good mood

Had a look ☐ Nearly there ☐ Nailed it ☐

Negative Charaktereigenschaften	*Negative personal characteristics*
angeberisch	pretentious
dickköpfig	stubborn
egoistisch*	egotistic, selfish
eingebildet	conceited
gemein*	mean, nasty
humorlos	humourless
neidisch	envious
peinlich	embarrassing
pessimistisch	pessimistic
rechthaberisch	bossy
selbstsüchtig*	selfish
stur	stubborn
verdorben	spoilt
verrückt	mad, crazy
verwöhnt	spoilt
schlechter Laune sein	to be in a bad mood

Had a look ☐ Nearly there ☐ Nailed it ☐

Beziehungen	*Relationships*
single	single
ledig	unmarried
unverheiratet	unmarried
verliebt	in love
verlobt	engaged
verheiratet	married
getrennt	separated
geschieden	divorced
sich verloben	to get engaged
heiraten	to get married
sich trennen	to separate, to split up
sich scheiden lassen	to get divorced
der/die Verlobte	fiancé(e)

Had a look ☐ Nearly there ☐ Nailed it ☐

Familie	*Family*
das Familienmitglied(er)	family member
der/die Verwandte	relative
der (Ehe-)Mann	husband
die (Ehe-)Frau	wife
die Großeltern	grandparents
der Opa(s)	grandpa
die Oma(s)	grandma
das Enkelkind(er)	grandchild
der Halbbruder(-brüder)	half-brother
die Stiefschwester(n)	stepsister
der Zwilling(e)	twin
der Onkel(-)	uncle
die Tante(n)	aunt
der Cousin(s)	(male) cousin
die Cousine(n)	(female) cousin
der/die Alleinerziehende	single parent
die Jugendlichen	young people, adolescents
der/die Erwachsene	adult
erwachsen	adult
adoptiert	adopted
aufpassen auf	to look after, to care for

Had a look ☐ Nearly there ☐ Nailed it ☐

Aussehen	*Appearance*
der Schnurrbart(-bärte)	moustache
eine Glatze haben	to be bald
altmodisch	old-fashioned
gepflegt	smart, neat
hässlich	ugly
schick	smart, chic
die Klamotten	clothes
die Mode	fashion
der Ohrring(e)	earring
Ich habe meinen eigenen Stil.	I have my own style.

Had a look ☐ Nearly there ☐ Nailed it ☐

Kapitel 3 Wörter

Freundschaften / *Friendships*
- der Einfluss / *influence*
- der Freundeskreis / *circle of friends*
- die Kommunikation / *communication*
- die Persönlichkeit / *character, personality*
- die Priorität(en) / *priority*
- der Streit(e) / *argument*
- der Typ / *guy, dude, bloke*
- die Unterstützung / *support*
- sich auf sich selbst konzentrieren / *to concentrate on yourself*
- gemeinsam / *together*
- kompliziert / *complicated*
- kommunizieren / *to communicate*
- plaudern / *to chat, to chatter*
- schwatzen / *to chat, to chatter*
- etwas vorhaben / *to have something planned*
- Wir mögen die gleichen Dinge. / *We like the same things.*

Had a look ☐ Nearly there ☐ Nailed it ☐

Meine perfekte Hochzeit / *My perfect wedding*
- das Büfett(s) / *buffet*
- die Gästeliste(n) / *guest list*
- das Hochzeitsmenü(s) / *wedding menu*
- der/die Hochzeitsplaner(in) / *wedding planner*
- das Programmheft(e) / *programme, order of service*
- der Tanzboden(–böden) / *dance floor*
- die Zeremonie(n) / *ceremony*
- versprechen / *to promise*
- seine Liebe beweisen / *to prove one's love*
- feierlich / *festive*
- luxuriös / *luxurious*

Had a look ☐ Nearly there ☐ Nailed it ☐

Probleme zu Hause / *Problems at home*
- ausbleiben / *to stay out*
- sich einmischen / *to interfere*
- lösen / *to solve, to resolve*
- die Lösung(en) / *solution*
- die Strategie(n) / *strategy*

Had a look ☐ Nearly there ☐ Nailed it ☐

K
3

 *Look for cognates and near-cognates when working out meanings of new words.

Treu looks very similar to 'true', which is a synonym for 'faithful'.

Optimistisch and *pessimistisch* should be easy to work out and can you see the link between *gemein* and 'mean', or *egoistisch* and 'selfish' (or 'egotistical')?

Kapitel 4 Wörter

Words I should know for speaking and writing activities

Zu Hause	**At home**
der Flur	hall
der Keller	cellar, basement
der Garten	garden
die Garage	garage
die Küche	kitchen
das Arbeitszimmer	study
das Badezimmer	bathroom
das Esszimmer	dining room
das Schlafzimmer	bedroom
das Wohnzimmer	sitting room
Ich wohne (seit vier Jahren) …	I have been living … (for four years).
in einer Kleinstadt	in a small town
in einer Großstadt	in a city
in der Stadtmitte	in the town centre
am Stadtrand	on the outskirts / in the suburbs
auf dem Land	in the countryside

Had a look ☐   Nearly there ☐   Nailed it ☐

das Einfamilienhaus	detached house
die Doppelhaushälfte	semi-detached house
das Reihenhaus	terraced house
das Hochhaus	high-rise building
der Wohnblock	block of flats
die 3-Zimmer-Wohnung	3-room flat
im zweiten Stock	on the second floor
im Untergeschoss	in the basement
im Erdgeschoss	on the ground floor
der Autostellplatz	parking space
der Dachboden	loft, attic
die Terrasse	terrace, patio

Had a look ☐   Nearly there ☐   Nailed it ☐

Essen und trinken	**Eating and drinking**
Es schmeckt …	It tastes …
lecker / köstlich / wunderbar	tasty / delicious / wonderful
würzig	spicy
ekelhaft / (un)appetitlich	disgusting / (un)appetising
geschmacklos	tasteless
scharf / sauer	hot, spicy / sour
salzig / fettig	salty / fatty
Ich esse (nicht) gern …	I (don't) like eating …
Ich esse lieber …	I prefer eating …
Ich esse am liebsten …	I like eating … best.
das Lieblingsessen	favourite meal
Ich bin Vegetarier(in).	I am vegetarian.
die Auswahl	choice, selection
auswählen	to choose
einkaufen	to buy, to shop
anklicken	to click on

vorbereiten	to prepare
eine leckere Spezialität aus …	a tasty speciality from …
das Frühstück	breakfast
das Mittagessen	lunch
das Abendbrot	dinner, evening meal
das Abendessen	dinner, evening meal
Das (Abendbrot) essen wir um …	We eat (dinner) at …

Had a look ☐   Nearly there ☐   Nailed it ☐

Zum Frühstück oder Abendessen	**For breakfast or dinner**
das Brot	bread
die Brotsorte	type of bread
das Brötchen	bread roll
die Butter	butter
der Käse	cheese
die Wurst	sausage
der Wurstaufschnitt	selection of sliced cold sausage
der Schinken	ham
das Ei (die Eier)	egg
das Spiegelei(er)	fried egg
der Lachs	salmon
die Marmelade	jam
der Honig	honey
der Pampelmusensaft	grapefruit juice
der Kräutertee	herbal tea
die Milch	milk
die fettarme Milch	skimmed milk
der Früchtetee	fruit tea
der Kaffee	coffee
der Saft	juice
das Glas Sekt	glass of champagne

Had a look ☐   Nearly there ☐   Nailed it ☐

Süßes und Nachspeisen	**Sweets and desserts**
die Nachspeise	dessert
das Eis	ice cream
das Gebäck	baked goods, pastries
das Mehl	flour
der Keks(e)	biscuit
die Torte(n)	gâteau
hausgemachte Torte(n)	home-made gâteau(x)
der Berliner	doughnut
der (Zucchini-)Kuchen	(courgette) cake
die Vanillesoße	vanilla sauce, custard
der Apfelstrudel	apple strudel
der Pflaumenkuchen	plum cake
mit Sahne	with cream

Had a look ☐   Nearly there ☐   Nailed it ☐

Kapitel 4 Wörter

Obst und Gemüse / *Fruit and vegetables*

das Obst	*fruit*
das Gemüse	*vegetables*
die Ananas(-)	*pineapple*
der Apfel (Äpfel)	*apple*
die Banane(n)	*banana*
die Birne(n)	*pear*
die Erdbeere(n)	*strawberry*
die Himbeere(n)	*raspberry*
die Kirsche(n)	*cherry*
die Orange(n)	*orange*
der Pfirsich(e)	*peach*
die Traube(n)	*grape*
die Zitrone(n)	*lemon*
der Blumenkohl(e)	*cauliflower*
die Erbse(n)	*pea*
die Gurke(n)	*cucumber*
die Karotte(n)	*carrot*
der Knoblauch	*garlic*
der Kohl(e)	*cabbage*
die Paprika(s)	*pepper*
die Tomate(n)	*tomato*
die Zwiebel(n)	*onion*

Had a look ☐ **Nearly there** ☐ **Nailed it** ☐

Auf Austausch / *On an exchange visit*

Herzlich willkommen!	*Welcome!*
Wie geht's dir / Ihnen?	*How are you?*
Wie war die Reise?	*How was the journey?*
Wie bitte?	*Pardon?*
Ich verstehe nicht.	*I don't understand.*
Hast du (die Hausschuhe) mitgebracht?	*Have you brought (slippers)?*
Können Sie bitte langsamer sprechen?	*Can you speak more slowly, please?*
Kannst du das bitte wiederholen?	*Can you repeat that, please?*
Hast du / Haben Sie Hunger?	*Are you hungry?*
Hast du / Haben Sie Durst?	*Are you thirsty?*
Hast du eine Frage an uns?	*Do you have a question for us?*
Was meinst du damit?	*What do you mean?*
Was bedeutet „Hausschuhe"?	*What does 'Hausschuhe' mean?*
Wie heißt „Wi-Fi-Code" auf Deutsch?	*How do you say 'WiFi code' in German?*
Was ist dein / Ihr „Wi-Fi-Code", bitte?	*What is your 'WiFi code', please?*

Had a look ☐ **Nearly there** ☐ **Nailed it** ☐

Man muss …	*We must …*
die Fahrräder unten im Keller abstellen	*put the bikes in the cellar*
die Treppen sauber halten	*keep the stairs clean*
den Müll ordentlich trennen	*separate the rubbish neatly*
in der Ruhezeit ruhig sein	*be quiet during 'quiet time'*
die Hausordnung	*house rules*
die Mittagsruhe	*quiet time at midday*
die Ruhezeit	*quiet time*
Man darf keine laute Musik spielen.	*We are not allowed to play loud music.*
Man darf kein Instrument üben.	*We are not allowed to practise an instrument.*
Man darf nicht mit dem Ball spielen.	*We are not allowed to play ball games.*
Man darf nie das Auto vor der Garage waschen.	*We are never allowed to wash the car in front of the garage.*
der Tagesablauf	*Daily routine*
an einem Schultag	*on a school day*
täglich	*daily*
während der Woche	*during the week*
am Abend / Nachmittag	*in the evening / afternoon*
zuerst	*first of all*
anschließend	*afterwards*
stundenlang	*for hours*
am Wochenende	*at the weekend*

Had a look ☐ **Nearly there** ☐ **Nailed it** ☐

Lebst du gesund? / *Are you healthy?*

Mein Lieblingssport ist …	*My favourite sport is …*
Fußball / Leichtathletik	*football / athletics*
Tennis / Turnen	*tennis / gymnastics*
Es macht Spaß.	*It's fun.*
Es ist gesund.	*It's healthy.*
Ich bin gern an der frischen Luft.	*I like being in the fresh air.*
Ich bin gern in einem Team.	*I like being in a team.*
Mein Vorbild ist …	*My role model is …*
ein(e) Athlet(in)	*an athlete*
ein(e) Fußballspieler(in)	*a footballer*
ein(e) Schwimmer(in)	*a swimmer*
ein(e) Tennisspieler(in)	*a tennis player*
Er/Sie …	*He/She …*
ist begabt	*is talented*
trainiert hart	*trains hard*
hat viele Medaillen gewonnen	*has won lots of medals*

Had a look ☐ **Nearly there** ☐ **Nailed it** ☐

Für meine Fitness …	*To keep fit …*
gehe ich joggen	*I go jogging*
gehe ich schwimmen	*I go swimming*
mache ich Muskeltraining	*I do weight training*
Ich esse sehr gesund.	*I eat very healthily.*

K4

Kapitel 4 Wörter

Ich esse ziemlich ungesund.	*I eat quite unhealthily.*	die Konsole	*console*
Ich esse Obst und Gemüse.	*I eat fruit and vegetables.*	das Handy	*mobile phone*
		die Kopfhörer (pl)	*headphones*
Ich mache eine gute Diät.	*I have a good diet.*	gefährlich	*dangerous*
		kreativ	*creative*
Ich esse täglich Fastfood.	*I eat fast food every day.*	praktisch	*practical*
		privat	*private*
das Gewicht	*weight*	schädlich	*harmful*
die Diät(en)	*diet*	sicher	*safe*
übergewichtig	*overweight*	spannend	*exciting*
abnehmen	*to lose weight*	süchtig	*addicted*
		teuer	*expensive*
		überraschend	*surprising*

Had a look ☐ Nearly there ☐ Nailed it ☐

Had a look ☐ Nearly there ☐ Nailed it ☐

Soziale Netzwerke und Technologie / *Social networks and technology*

Vor- und Nachteile der Technologie / *Advantages and disadvantages of technology*

simsen	*to text*	Ein großer Vorteil der Technologie ist, dass …	*A big advantage of technology is that …*
eine SMS schicken / senden	*to send a text*	Der größte Vorteil ist, dass …	*The biggest advantage is that …*
per Handy / Internet telefonieren	*to call on a mobile / via the internet*	Ein großer Nachteil ist, dass …	*A big disadvantage is that …*
soziale Netzwerke nutzen	*to use social networks*	Der größte Nachteil ist, dass …	*The biggest disadvantage is that …*
online / im Internet chatten	*to chat online*	Das Gute daran ist, dass …	*The good thing about it is that …*
im Internet surfen	*to surf online*	Das Beste daran ist, dass …	*The best thing about it is that …*
Fotos hochladen	*to upload photos*	Schlecht daran ist, dass …	*What's bad about it is that …*
Musik herunterladen	*to download music*	Es gibt mehr Vorteile als Nachteile.	*There are more advantages than disadvantages.*
sich mit Freunden unterhalten	*to chat with friends*	einerseits … andererseits	*on the one hand … on the other hand*
E-Mails schreiben	*to write emails*	auf der einen Seite	*on the one hand*
Briefe tippen	*to type letters*	auf der anderen Seite	*on the other hand*
einen Kommentar schreiben	*to write a comment*	im Großen und Ganzen	*by and large*

Had a look ☐ Nearly there ☐ Nailed it ☐

der Bildschirm	*screen*
der Desktop-PC	*desktop computer / PC*
die Digitalkamera	*digital camera*
der MP3-Player	*MP3 player*
der Musik-Streaming-Dienst	*music streaming service*
das Smart-TV	*Smart TV*
das Tablet	*tablet*

Vor allem ist das positiv, weil … — *Above all, that is positive because …*

Das Internet kann zu Problemen führen. — *The internet can lead to problems.*

Had a look ☐ Nearly there ☐ Nailed it ☐

Kapitel 4 Wörter

Extra words I should know for reading and listening activities

Wo ich wohne	**Where I live**
die Eigentumswohnung(en)	owner-occupied flat
das Privatbad	private/ensuite bathroom
das Waschbecken	washbasin
der Schreibtisch	desk
die Etage(n)	floor, storey
das Gebäude(-)	building
der Bauernhof(–höfe)	farm
der/die Mitbewohner(in)	fellow occupant, house / flat mate
der Rasen	lawn
mieten	to rent
renoviert	renovated
nebenan	next door

Had a look ☐   Nearly there ☐   Nailed it ☐

Die Tagesroutine	**Daily routine**
Ich frühstücke.	I have breakfast.
Ich gehe ins Bett.	I go to bed.
Ich setze mich an den Computer.*	I sit down at the computer.
Ich amüsiere mich.	I enjoy myself.
Ich langweile mich.	I get bored.
Ich treffe mich mit Freunden.	I meet friends.
das Alltagsleben	daily life
im Freien spielen	to play in the open air
den Tisch decken	to lay the table

Had a look ☐   Nearly there ☐   Nailed it ☐

Essen und trinken	**Eating and drinking**
die Mahlzeit(en)	meal
die Geburtstagstorte	birthday cake
pikant	spicy
gedämpft	steamed
gedünstet	steamed
gekocht	boiled, cooked
hausgemacht	home-made
das Getränk(e)	drink
die Flasche(n)	bottle
das Glas (Gläser)	jar, glass

die Packung(en)	packet
die Scheibe(n)	slice
das Stück(e)	piece
die Tasse(n)	cup
die Schüssel(n)	bowl
das Messer(–)	knife
die Gabel(n)	fork
der Löffel(–)	spoon
der Teelöffel(–)	teaspoon
die Serviette(n)	napkin
die Platte(n)	platter

Had a look ☐   Nearly there ☐   Nailed it ☐

Lebst du gesund?	**Are you healthy?**
der Lebensstil(e)	lifestyle
der Dauerglotzer(–)	couch potato
rauchen	to smoke
Alkohol trinken	to drink alcohol
leiden (an)	to suffer (from)
die Allergie(n)	allergy
das psychologische Problem(e)	psychological problem
depressiv	depressive
gestresst	stressed
arm	poor
sich gesund ernähren	to have a healthy diet
das Fastfood	fast food
das Fertiggericht(e)	ready meal
das Milchprodukt(e)	dairy product
verdünnt	diluted
das Muskeltraining	weight training
der Triathlon(e)	triathlon
diszipliniert	disciplined
schaffen	to manage

Had a look ☐   Nearly there ☐   Nailed it ☐

K4

Kapitel 4 Wörter

Technologie	Technology
der Blickkontakt	eye contact
persönliche Daten (pl)	personal information
der Drucker(-)	printer
die Gefahr(en)	danger
das persönliche Gespräch(e)	face-to-face conversation
das Internet-Mobbing	cyberbullying
die Körpersprache	body language
die Maus (Mäuse)	mouse
das Risiko (Risiken)	risk
die Sicherheit	security
die Tastatur(en)	keyboard
die Verbindung(en)	connection
sich ausdrücken	to express oneself
in Kontakt bleiben	to stay in contact
brennen	to burn
drucken	to print
laden	to load
löschen	to erase, to delete
absaven	to save, to store
sichern	to save, to store
speichern	to save, to store
per Festnetz telefonieren	to phone via landline
tippen	to type

Had a look ☐   **Nearly there** ☐   **Nailed it** ☐

---

*Check which case is used with the verbs *sich setzen* and *sitzen* to ensure you interpret the correct meaning:

*Ich setze mich **an den** Computer.* (movement – accusative)

I **sit down** at the computer.

*Ich sitze **am** Computer.* (no movement – dative)

I **sit** at the computer.

Kapitel 5 Wörter

Words I should know for speaking and writing activities

Verkehrsmittel	**Forms of transport**
Ich fahre …	I travel …
mit dem Zug / Bus / Auto / Rad	by train / bus / car / bike
mit der U-Bahn / S-Bahn / Straßenbahn	by underground / urban railway / tram
Ich fliege mit dem Flugzeug.	I travel by plane.
Ich fliege.	I fly.
Ich gehe zu Fuß.	I go on foot. / I walk.

Had a look ☐ Nearly there ☐ Nailed it ☐

Hotelzimmer reservieren	**Booking hotel rooms**
Ich möchte … reservieren.	I would like to reserve …
ein Einzelzimmer	a single room
zwei Doppelzimmer	two double rooms
ein Zimmer mit Aussicht	a room with a view
für eine Nacht	for one night
für zwei Nächte vom 8. bis 10. November	for two nights from 8 to 10 November
Gibt es WLAN im Hotel?	Is there Wi-Fi in the hotel?
der Fitnessraum (–räume)	gym
der Parkplatz(–plätze)	car park, parking space
das Restaurant(s)	restaurant
Darf ich den Hund zum Hotel mitbringen?	Can I bring my dog with me to the hotel?
Um wie viel Uhr ist das Frühstück / Abendessen?	What time is breakfast / dinner?
Wie viel kostet das Zimmer?	How much is the room?

Had a look ☐ Nearly there ☐ Nailed it ☐

Fahrkarten kaufen	**Buying train tickets**
Ich möchte eine Fahrkarte nach Berlin, bitte.	I'd like a ticket to Berlin, please.
Einfach oder hin und zurück?	Single or return?
Wann fährt der nächste Zug ab?	When does the next train leave?
Er fährt um 12:51 Uhr vom Gleis 22 ab.	It leaves at 12:51 from platform 22.
Wann kommt er an?	When does it arrive?
Er kommt in Berlin um 19:18 Uhr an.	It arrives in Berlin at 19:18.
Fährt der Zug direkt oder muss ich umsteigen?	Does the train go direct or do I need to change?

Had a look ☐ Nearly there ☐ Nailed it ☐

Ferienunterkunft	**Holiday accommodation**
das Hotel(s)	hotel
das Gasthaus(–häuser)	guest house / bed and breakfast
die Ferienwohnung(en)	holiday apartment
die Jugendherberge(n)	youth hostel
der Campingplatz (–plätze)	campsite
Ich würde am liebsten (in diesem Hotel) übernachten.	I would like best to stay (in this hotel).
in der Stadtmitte / im Stadtzentrum	in the town centre
am Stadtrand	in the suburbs / outskirts
am nächsten (zum Bahnhof)	nearest (to the station)
(Der Bahnhof) liegt (100 m) entfernt.	(The station) is (100 m) away.

Had a look ☐ Nearly there ☐ Nailed it ☐

der Computerraum (–räume)	computer room
der Fernsehraum (–räume)	TV room
der Garten (Gärten)	garden
der Spieleraum(–räume)	games room
der Supermarkt (–märkte)	supermarket
der Waschsalon(s)	launderette
die Klimaanlage(n)	air conditioning
das Freibad(–bäder) mit Sauna	open-air pool with sauna
Er/Sie/Es ist … / sieht … aus.	It is / looks …
modern	modern
praktisch	practical / handy
ruhig	quiet
altmodisch	old-fashioned
chaotisch	chaotic
schmutzig	dirty
(un)bequem	(un)comfortable

Had a look ☐ Nearly there ☐ Nailed it ☐

Urlaubsbeschwerden	**Holiday complaints**
Das Zimmer war klein und schmutzig.	The room was small and dirty.
Es waren lange Haare in der Dusche / im Waschbecken.	There were long hairs in the shower / in the washbasin.
Ich war total unzufrieden.	I was totally dissatisfied.
Ich werde nie wieder in diesem Hotel übernachten.	I will never stay in this hotel again.

K5

Kapitel 5 Wörter

Dieses Gasthaus hatte keinen Internetanschluss.	This guest house had no internet connection.	Kannst du / Können Sie mir helfen?	Can you help me?
Es gab keine Klimaanlage.	There was no air conditioning.	Entschuldige / Entschuldigen Sie.	Excuse me.
Das Frühstück war ein Höhepunkt.	Breakfast was a highlight.	Wo ist der / die / das …?	Where is the …?
Es gab Renovierungsarbeiten.	There were renovation works.	Had a look ☐ Nearly there ☐ Nailed it ☐	
Es gab viel Lärm.	There was a lot of noise.	**Die Speisekarte**	**Menu**
Unser Zelt war direkt neben dem Spieleraum / Waschsalon.	Our tent was right next to the games room / launderette.	die Vorspeise(n)	starter
		die Hauptspeise(n)	main course
		die Nachspeise(n)	dessert
Jede Nacht haben wir den Fernseher / die Discomusik / die Waschmaschinen gehört.	Every night we heard the TV / disco music / the washing machines.	die Beilage(n)	side dish
		die Getränkekarte(n)	drinks menu
		das Tagesgericht(e)	dish of the day
		Bedienung inbegriffen	service included
Had a look ☐ Nearly there ☐ Nailed it ☐		gefüllt	filled, stuffed
		gemischt	mixed
Wegbeschreibungen	**Directions**	geröstet	roast
Fahr / Fahren Sie …	Go … (using a vehicle)	hausgemacht	homemade
Geh / Gehen Sie …	Go … (walking)	das Bier vom Fass	draught beer
rechts / links / geradeaus	right / left / straight on	der Fruchtsaft	fruit juice
		der Wein	wine
weiter bis zum/zur …	further until …	Had a look ☐ Nearly there ☐ Nailed it ☐	
über …	over …		
Nimm / Nehmen Sie …	Take …	**Im Restaurant**	**In the restaurant**
die erste / zweite Straße links	the first / second road on the left	Wir möchten einen Tisch … haben.	We'd like a table …
Bieg / Biegen Sie an der Ecke rechts ab.	Turn right at the corner.	für (vier) Personen	for (four) people
		mit Aussicht auf die Donau	with a view of the Danube
Überquer / Überqueren Sie …	Cross …	in der Ecke	in the corner
die Ampel(n)	the traffic lights	hier links	on the left here
den Platz (Plätze)	the square	Könnte ich bitte (die Speisekarte / Getränkekarte) haben?	Could I have (the menu / drinks menu), please?
die Brücke(n)	the bridge		
die Donau	the Danube		
die Kreuzung(en)	crossroads	Das Tagesgericht ist …	The dish of the day is …
Had a look ☐ Nearly there ☐ Nailed it ☐		Had a look ☐ Nearly there ☐ Nailed it ☐	
das Rathaus(–häuser)	town hall	**Restaurant-beschwerden**	**Restaurant complaints**
der Rathausplatz (–plätze)	town hall square	Ich möchte mich beschweren!	I would like to make a complaint!
das Museum (Museen)	museum	Dieser Löffel ist schmutzig.	This spoon is dirty.
die Oper(n)	opera house		
Es ist hundert Meter entfernt.	It's one hundred metres away.	Es ist ein Haar in diesem Salat.	There's a hair in this salad.
Es ist auf der rechten Seite.	It's on the right.	Dieser Tisch … ist sehr laut	This table … is very noisy
Kannst du / Können Sie …	Can you …	hat keine Aussicht	has no view
mir sagen, wie ich zum / zur… komme?	tell me how to get to …?	ist in der dunkelsten Ecke	is in the darkest corner
mir den Weg zum / zur … zeigen?	show me the way to …?	Das Bier ist zu warm.	The beer is too warm.
Ich habe mich verlaufen.	I'm lost.	Dieser Wurstteller war sehr fettig.	This sausage platter was very fatty.

32

Kapitel 5 Wörter

Das war (die schrecklichste Suppe). / That was (the most terrible soup).
Ich konnte (das Tagesgericht) nicht essen, weil es … war. / I couldn't eat (the dish of the day) because it was …

Had a look ☐ Nearly there ☐ Nailed it ☐

Souvenirs / Souvenirs

der Kuli(s) / ballpoint pen
der Schmuck / jewellery
die Brieftasche(n) / wallet
das Portemonnaie(s) / purse
die Tasse(n) / mug, cup
das Bild(er) / picture
das Kopfkissen(–) / pillow, cushion
das Tischtuch(–tücher) / table cloth
der Keks(e) / biscuit
bunt / multi-coloured
(grün-weiß) gestreift / (green and white) striped
preiswert / inexpensive, good value
weich / soft

Had a look ☐ Nearly there ☐ Nailed it ☐

Einkaufen / Shopping

der Markt (Märkte) / market
der Souvenirladen (–läden) / souvenir shop
das Kaufhaus(–häuser) / department store
das Einkaufszentrum (–zentren) / shopping centre
Ich suche (ein T-Shirt) als Geschenk für (meinen Bruder). / I'm looking for (a T-shirt) as a present for (my brother).
Welche Größe hat (er)? / What size is (he)?
klein / mittelgroß / groß / small / medium / large
Seine Lieblingsfarben sind … / His favourite colours are …
altmodisch / old-fashioned
beliebt / popular
kaputt / broken
kurz / lang / short / long
preiswert / inexpensive, good value
schmutzig / dirty
teuer / expensive
im Sonderangebot / on special offer
… funktioniert nicht / … doesn't work
… passt mir nicht / … doesn't fit me
… hat ein Loch / … has a hole

Had a look ☐ Nearly there ☐ Nailed it ☐

Ein Problem melden / Reporting a problem

Mir ist schlecht / kalt. / I feel ill / cold.
Das Bein tut mir weh. / My leg hurts.
Ich habe mir den Arm verletzt. / I have injured my arm.
Ich möchte einen Handy-Diebstahl melden. / I'd like to report a mobile phone theft.
(Meine Mutter) ist auf dem Bürgersteig gefallen. / (My mother) fell over on the pavement.
Ich möchte mich über (die Toiletten) beschweren. / I'd like to complain about (the toilets).
Ich suche einen Geldautomaten. / I'm looking for a cash point.
Ich habe (meine Schlüssel / meine Brieftasche) verloren. / I have lost (my keys / my wallet).
Ich habe meinen Rucksack (im Café) gelassen. / I left my rucksack (in the café).
Gibt es hier in der Nähe ein Fundbüro / eine Apotheke? / Is there a lost-property office / chemist near here?
Sie müssen / Du musst … / You must …
zur Polizeiwache gehen / go to the police station
zum Fundbüro gehen / go to the lost-property office
ins Krankenhaus gehen / go to hospital
das Formular ausfüllen / fill in the form
Ich werde es dem Manager sagen. / I will tell the manager.
Ich werde einen Krankenwagen rufen. / I will call an ambulance.

Had a look ☐ Nearly there ☐ Nailed it ☐

In der Apotheke / At the chemist's

Ich habe Kopfweh. / I have a headache.
Ich leide unter Migräne. / I suffer from migraines.
Ich habe Zahnschmerzen. / I have a toothache.
Ich habe mir den Arm verletzt. / I have injured my arm.
Ich bin müde / erschöpft. / I am tired / exhausted.
Ich habe Husten. / I have a cough.
Ich habe Halsschmerzen. / I have a sore throat.
Sie müssen / könnten … / You must / could …
Tabletten / Vitamine / Hustenbonbons nehmen / take tablets / vitamins / throat sweets
eine Salbe benutzen / use an ointment
beim Zahnarzt anrufen / call the dentist
einen Termin ausmachen / make an appointment
ins Krankenhaus gehen / go to hospital

Had a look ☐ Nearly there ☐ Nailed it ☐

K5

Kapitel 5 Wörter

Extra words I should know for reading and listening activities

Unterwegs — *On the move*
der Bahnsteig(e)	platform
der Bürgersteig(e)	pavement
die Bushaltestelle(n)	bus stop
der Fahrkartenschalter(-)	ticket counter
das Fahrzeug(e)	vehicle
der Fußgänger(-)	pedestrian
der Fußgängerübergang (-gänge)	pedestrian crossing
der Kreisverkehr(-)	roundabout (traffic)
die Linie	line
das Mofa(s)	moped
das Motorrad(-räder)	motorbike
der Reisebus(-busse)	coach
die Route	route
die Umleitung(en)	diversion
der Wartesaal(-säle)	waiting room
der Wohnwagen(-)	caravan

Had a look ☐   Nearly there ☐   Nailed it ☐

Mit dem Zug fahren — *Travelling by train*
die Bahnkarte(n)	railcard
die Ermäßigung(en)	reduction
der Fahrplan(-pläne)	timetable
das Gepäck	luggage
die Seniorenkarte(n)	senior citizen card
die Verspätung(en)	delay
besetzt	occupied, taken (seat)
umweltfreundlich	environmentally friendly
einsteigen*	to get on (bus, train, etc.)
aussteigen*	to get off (bus, train, etc.)

Had a look ☐   Nearly there ☐   Nailed it ☐

Unterkunft — *Accommodation*
die Pension(en)	bed and breakfast
die Halbpension	half board
die Vollpension	full board
das Lokal(e)	pub
das Hotelpersonal	hotel staff
der Empfangschef/die Empfangsdame	receptionist
der Aufenthaltsraum (-räume)	common room, lounge
der Aufzug(-züge)	lift
der Fahrstuhl(-stühle)	lift
das Zweibettzimmer	twin room
die Reservierung(en)	reservation
die Anmeldung	registration, booking in
der Aufenthalt	stay
der Rabatt(e)	discount

Had a look ☐   Nearly there ☐   Nailed it ☐

Beschwerden — *Complaints*
die Bettwäsche	bed linen
der Schlafsack(-säcke)	sleeping bag
die Heizung	heating
der Koffer(-)	suitcase
sich beklagen	to complain
sich beschweren	to complain
bemängeln	to find fault with
zelten	to camp
bestätigen	to confirm
ungenügend	unsatisfactory
im Voraus	in advance

Had a look ☐   Nearly there ☐   Nailed it ☐

Rund um die Stadt — *Around town*
der Alptraum	nightmare
der Ausgang(-gänge)	exit
der Besucher(-)	visitor
der Eingang(-gänge)	entrance
der Eintritt	entry, admission (to place / event)
die Eintrittskarte(n)	entry / admission ticket
die Kneipe	pub
das Nachtleben	nightlife
die Öffnungszeiten	opening times
die Richtung	direction
die Rundfahrt(en)	tour (on transport)
der Rundgang(-gänge)	tour (walking)
der Schnellimbiss(e)	snack (bar)
der Stadtplan(-pläne)	town plan, map
der Unfall	accident
das Verkehrsamt	tourist information office
sehenswert	worth seeing
sich verlaufen**	to get lost

Had a look ☐   Nearly there ☐   Nailed it ☐

---

*Look carefully at small words at the start of verbs which can change their meaning:
- einsteigen   to get in/on   Ich **steige** in den Bus **ein**.
- aussteigen   to get out/off   Er **steigt** aus dem Zug **aus**.
- umsteigen   to change (e.g. trains)   Wir **steigen** in Köln **um**.

**'To get lost' in German is *sich verlaufen*. Don't fall into the trap of using the verb *verlieren*.
Ich habe mich in der Stadtmitte verlaufen.
I got lost in the town centre.

Words I should know for speaking and writing activities

Länder und Orte	**Countries and places**
im Ausland	abroad
Bayern	Bavaria
die Ostsee	the Baltic Sea
die Nordsee	the North Sea
Spanien	Spain
Italien	Italy
die Türkei	Turkey
Österreich	Austria
Kroatien	Croatia
Frankreich	France
die Schweiz	Switzerland
Großbritannien	Great Britain
Griechenland	Greece
Ich fahre / reise / fliege …	I go / travel / fly …
nach Deutschland	to Germany
in die Türkei	to Turkey
an einen See	to a lake
an das (ans) Meer	to the sea
an den Strand	to the beach / seaside
an die Küste	to the coast
auf eine Insel	to an island
in den Wald	to the forest / woods
in die Berge	to the mountains

Had a look ☐ Nearly there ☐ Nailed it ☐

Himmelsrichtungen	**Points of the compass**
der Kompass	compass
der Norden	north
der Nordosten	north east
der Osten	east
der Südosten	south east
der Süden	south
der Südwesten	south west
der Westen	west
der Nordwesten	north west
in der Mitte	in the middle

Had a look ☐ Nearly there ☐ Nailed it ☐

Das Wetter	**The weather**
Es ist …	It is …
heiß	hot
kalt	cold
sonnig	sunny
trocken	dry
regnerisch	rainy
windig	windy
wolkig	cloudy
neblig	foggy
frostig	frosty
stürmisch	stormy
wechselhaft	changeable
Es …	It's …
friert	freezing
hagelt	hailing
regnet	raining
schneit	snowing

Had a look ☐ Nearly there ☐ Nailed it ☐

Es gibt …	There is (are) …
Nebel	fog
Regen(–schauer)	rain (showers)
einen Sturm	a storm
ein Gewitter	a thunderstorm
Die Temperaturen liegen zwischen (15) und (18) Grad.	Temperatures lie between (15) and (18) degrees.
Die Temperatur ist hoch / niedrig.	The temperature is high / low.
Es wird windig / neblig sein.	It will be windy / foggy.
Es wird frieren / regnen / schneien.	It will freeze / rain / snow.
Es wird … geben.	There will be …
(keinen) Regen	(no) rain
(keine) Wolken	(no) clouds

Had a look ☐ Nearly there ☐ Nailed it ☐

Die Jahreszeiten	**The seasons**
der Frühling / das Frühjahr	spring
der Sommer	summer
der Herbst	autumn
der Winter	winter

Had a look ☐ Nearly there ☐ Nailed it ☐

Urlaubsarten	**Types of holidays**
Ich mache (nicht) gern …	I (don't) like …
Pauschalurlaub	a package holiday
Aktivurlaub	an active holiday
Erlebnisurlaub	an adventure holiday
Strandurlaub	a beach holiday
Winterurlaub	a winter holiday
Sightseeingurlaub	a sightseeing holiday
Urlaub auf Balkonien	a staycation, a holiday at home
Ich gehe (nicht) gern zelten, weil ich …	I (don't) like going camping because I …
abenteuerlustig bin	am adventurous
gern draußen bin	like being outdoors
gern in der Sonne liege	like sunbathing
gern andere Kulturen erlebe	like experiencing other cultures
mich für die Natur interessiere	am interested in nature

Kapitel 6 Wörter

mich entspannen will	want to relax	die Feier	the party
mich schnell langweile	get bored easily	das Wochenende	the weekend
nichts tun will	don't want to do anything	Meine Freunde hatten ... gekauft.	My friends had bought ...

Had a look ☐ Nearly there ☐ Nailed it ☐

das Essen / die Getränke / Luftballons — the food / the drinks / balloons
Wir haben (gefeiert / getanzt / gegessen). — We (celebrated / danced / ate).
Ich war (zum Bahnhof) gefahren. — I had gone (to the station).
Ich hatte (mein Handy) vergessen. — I had forgotten (my mobile phone).

Wie war der Urlaub? / How was the holiday?

Die Reise ...	The journey ...
war furchtbar	was awful
hat ewig gedauert	lasted forever
Wir mussten stundenlang im Auto sitzen.	We had to sit in the car for hours.
Es gab einen Stau auf der Autobahn.	There was a traffic jam on the motorway.
Wir haben uns die ganze Zeit gestritten.	We argued / quarrelled the whole time.
Der Zug hatte Verspätung.	The train was delayed.
Das Bad war dreckig.	The bath was dirty.
Die Dusche hat nicht funktioniert.	The shower didn't work.
Die Ferienwohnung war ...	The holiday apartment was ...
gut eingerichtet	well-furnished
sehr sauber	very clean

Had a look ☐ Nearly there ☐ Nailed it ☐

Urlaubsartikel / Holiday items

das Visum	visa
die Buchungsbestätigung	booking confirmation
der Reisepass	passport
die Medikamente	medicines
der Führerschein	driving licence
der Jugendherbergsausweis	youth hostel membership card
die Reise-Apps	travel apps
der Personalausweis	identity card

Had a look ☐ Nearly there ☐ Nailed it ☐

Während des Urlaubs ...	During the holiday ...
sind wir in den Bergen wandern gegangen	we went walking in the mountains
war das Wetter wunderschön	the weather was beautiful
hat es jeden Tag geregnet	it rained every day
Wir haben den Urlaub genossen.	We enjoyed the holiday.
Die Landschaft war sehr schön.	The scenery was very beautiful.
Das Essen hat mir sehr gut geschmeckt.	I really liked the food.
außerhalb	outside of
innerhalb	inside, within
statt	instead of
trotz	in spite of
während	during
wegen	because of

Had a look ☐ Nearly there ☐ Nailed it ☐

Absichten äußern / Expressing intentions

planen	to plan
hoffen	to hope
Lust haben	to be keen
vorhaben	to intend
um ... zu	in order to
ohne ... zu	without

Had a look ☐ Nearly there ☐ Nailed it ☐

Wenn ... / If ...

Wenn ich mehr Geld / mehr Zeit / keine (Flug-)Angst hätte, ...	If I had more money / more time / no fear (of flying), ...
Wenn ich mutiger / reicher wäre, ... würde ich ...	If I were braver / richer ... I would ...
nach Australien / zum Mond fliegen	fly to Australia / to the moon
auf Safari gehen	go on safari
in einem Luxushotel übernachten	stay in a luxury hotel

Had a look ☐ Nearly there ☐ Nailed it ☐

Eine Feier organisieren / Organising a party

Mein Freund hatte mich zur Party in ... eingeladen.	My friend had invited me to the party in ...
Ich hatte ... organisiert.	I had organised ...
den Urlaub	the holiday

Wo ich wohne / Where I live

Es gibt einen Flughafen / Bahnhof.	There is an airport / a station.
Es gab keine Autobahn / Schule / Universität.	There was no motorway / school / university.

Kapitel 6 Wörter

Es wird ... geben.	There will be ...
ein Fußballstadion / Kino	a football stadium / cinema
Fußgängerzonen / Touristen	pedestrian precincts / tourists
Leuchttürme / Museen	lighthouses / museums
nicht so viele Autos	not so many cars

Had a look ☐ **Nearly there** ☐ **Nailed it** ☐

Meine Stadt: Vor- und Nachteile
My town: advantages and disadvantages

Ich wohne in einer Stadt / in einem Vorort, wo ...	I live in a town / suburb where ...
man (Lebensmittel) kaufen kann	you can buy (groceries)
es (eine Bäckerei) gibt	there's a (bakery)
ich überall zu Fuß hinkomme	I can get everywhere on foot
ich mich nie langweile	I never get bored
es oft zu laut ist	it is often too noisy
es zu viel Verkehr / Müll gibt	there is too much traffic / rubbish
Es gibt in der Umgebung ...	In the neighbourhood there is ...
fast nichts für junge Leute	virtually nothing for young people
ein vielseitiges Kulturangebot	a varied cultural offering

Had a look ☐ **Nearly there** ☐ **Nailed it** ☐

Wir haben früher ... gewohnt.	Before, we lived ...
in einer Kleinstadt / Großstadt	in a small town / city
außerhalb der Stadt	outside the town
Es gab weder Freibad noch Tennisplatz.	There was neither an open-air pool nor a tennis court.
Man sollte / könnte ...	We should / could ...
vielseitige Aktivitäten für Jugendliche anbieten	offer varied activities for young people
neue Parkplätze am Stadtrand bauen	build new car parks on the outskirts of the town
die öffentlichen Verkehrsmittel verbessern	improve public transport
mehr Wohnungen bauen	build more flats
mehr Fahrradwege haben	have more cycle paths
Autos in der Innenstadt verbieten, um Staus zu reduzieren	ban cars from the town centre to reduce traffic jams
die Straßen sauber halten	keep the streets clean

Had a look ☐ **Nearly there** ☐ **Nailed it** ☐

K 6

Kapitel 6 Wörter

Extra words I should know for reading and listening activities

Urlaubsplanung / *Planning holidays*

das Boot(e)	*boat*
die Fähre(n)	*ferry*
die Seilbahn(en)	*cable car*
das Wohnmobil(e)*	*camper van*
die Vorbereitung(en)	*preparation*
die Landkarte(n)	*map*
der Abstecher(–)	*detour*
die Hauptsaison	*high season*
inklusive	*included*
im Angebot	*on offer*
bezahlbar	*affordable*
vorher	*before(hand)*
bieten	*to offer*
buchen	*to book*
zur Verfügung stehen	*to be available*

Had a look ☐ Nearly there ☐ Nailed it ☐

Meine Gegend / *My area*

die Aufregung	*excitement*
das Gebiet(e)	*area*
die Geschwindigkeit	*speed*
die Geschwindig-keitsbegrenzung	*speed limit*
die Grünanlage(n)	*green space, park*
die Industrie(n)	*industry*
die Landwirtschaft	*agriculture*
der Lastwagen(–)	*lorry*
die Raststätte(n)	*motorway services*
der Stadtteil(e)	*part of town*
das Stadtviertel(–)	*district, quarter (of a town)*
die Stoßzeit	*rush hour*
der Vorort(e)	*suburb*

Had a look ☐ Nearly there ☐ Nailed it ☐

Im Urlaub / *On holiday*

baden	*to swim, bathe*
die Ausstellung(en)	*exhibition*
die Autovermietung	*car hire*
der Badeort(e)*	*seaside resort, spa*
die Eishalle(n)	*ice rink*
der Fahrradverleih	*bike hire*
das Festland	*mainland*
der Hafen (Häfen)	*port*
der Laden (Läden)	*shop*
die Lage(n)	*situation, position*
der Spielplatz(–plätze)	*playground*
die Sportanlagen (pl)	*sports facilities*
das Tal (Täler)	*valley*
der Tourismus	*tourism*
die Unterhaltungs-möglichkeiten	*entertainment opportunities, things to do*
die Veranstaltung(en)	*event*
einen Sonnenbrand bekommen	*to get sunburnt*
erholsam	*restful*
Schlittschuh laufen	*to go ice skating*
entdecken	*to discover*

Had a look ☐ Nearly there ☐ Nailed it ☐

Das Wetter / *The weather*

das Klima	*climate*
die Wettervorhersage	*weather forecast*
die Höchsttemperatur	*highest temperature*
die Tiefsttemperatur	*lowest temperature*
die Durchschnitts-temperatur	*average temperature*
steigen	*to rise (temperature)*
heiter	*bright*
bedeckt	*overcast*
aufklären	*to brighten up*
die Aufheiterung(en)	*bright spell*
der Niederschlag	*precipitation, rainfall*

Had a look ☐ Nearly there ☐ Nailed it ☐

⭐ *To work out the meaning of a new word, ask yourself if it is similar to one you already know, and if it contains cognates or near-cognates:*

das Wohnmobil → *wohnen* (to live) + *mobil* (mobile) = 'mobile home', or 'camper van'

der Badeort → *baden* (to swim / bathe) + *Ort* (place) = 'swimming place' or 'seaside resort'

Remember to think beyond the literal translation when working out the correct English meaning.

Kapitel 7 Wörter

Words I should know for speaking and writing activities

Berufe	Jobs
der/die Anwalt/Anwältin	lawyer
der/die Apotheker(in)	chemist
der/die Architekt(in)	architect
der/die Arzt/Ärztin	doctor
der/die Bäcker(in)	baker
der/die Bankangestellte	bank clerk
der/die Beamte/Beamtin	civil servant
der/die Bibliothekar(in)	librarian
der/die Chef(in)	boss
der/die Dolmetscher(in)	interpreter
der/die Elektriker(in)	electrician
der/die Feuerwehrmann/-frau	firefighter
der/die Friseur/Friseuse	hairdresser
der/die Informatiker(in)	computer scientist
der/die Journalist(in)	journalist
der/die Kellner(in)	waiter/waitress
der/die Klempner(in)	plumber
der/die Koch/Köchin	cook
der/die Kraftfahrer(in)	lorry driver
der/die Krankenpfleger/ Krankenschwester	nurse

Had a look ☐ Nearly there ☐ Nailed it ☐

der/die Lehrer(in)	teacher
der/die Manager(in)	manager
der/die Mechaniker(in)	mechanic
der/die Metzger(in)	butcher
der/die Pilot(in)	pilot
der/die Polizist(in)	police officer
der/die Programmierer(in)	computer programmer
der/die Schauspieler(in)	actor/actress
der/die Sozialarbeiter(in)	social worker
der/die Tierarzt/Tierärztin	vet
der/die Verkäufer(in)	sales assistant
der/die Steward(ess)	air steward(ess)
der/die Übersetzer(in)	translator

Had a look ☐ Nearly there ☐ Nailed it ☐

Arbeitsorte	Places of work
der Keller(-)	cellar
der Laden (Läden)	shop
die Apotheke(n)	chemist's
die Autowerkstatt (-stätten)	garage
die Bäckerei(en)	bakery
die Bank(en)	bank
die Metzgerei(en)	butcher's

die Polizeiwache(n)	police station
das Büro(s)	office
das Flugzeug(e)	aeroplane
das Geschäft(e)	shop
das Krankenhaus (-häuser)	hospital
das Labor(s)	laboratory
das Reisebüro(s)	travel agency
das Restaurant(s)	restaurant
das Theater(-)	theatre

Had a look ☐ Nearly there ☐ Nailed it ☐

Ein Praktikum	A work experience
Beim Arbeitspraktikum musste ich ...	For my work experience I had to ...
Glücklicherweise musste ich keine ...	Fortunately I didn't have to ...
Telefonanrufe machen	make phone calls
Akten / Dokumente abheften	file files / documents
Formulare ausfüllen	fill in forms
E-Mails schreiben	write emails
Gäste bedienen	serve customers
Autos waschen	wash cars
Termine organisieren	organise meetings
Ich musste auch (keinen) ...	I also did (not) have to ...
Tee / Kaffee machen	make tea / coffee

Had a look ☐ Nearly there ☐ Nailed it ☐

Berufsbilder	Job descriptions
Sie haben ausgezeichnete ...	You have an excellent ...
Deutschkenntnisse	knowledge of German
Sprachkenntnisse	knowledge of languages
Sie sind in (Deutsch) fließend.	You are fluent in (German).
Sie müssen hervorragende Kommunikationsfähigkeiten haben.	You need to have excellent communication skills.
Sie sind für die technischen Aspekte verantwortlich.	You are responsible for the technical aspects.
Sie beschäftigen sich mit (Strom).	You deal with (electricity).
Sie ... schreiben Reportagen	You ... write reports
decken Skandale auf	uncover scandals
berichten über viele aktuelle Themen	report on lots of current issues
interviewen (die Stars)	interview (the stars)
Sie müssen ...	You must ...
zuverlässig sein	be reliable

K 7

39

Kapitel 7 Wörter

Ihre Arbeit pünktlich abliefern	deliver your work on time	gehe ich zum Sportverein	I have been going to a sports club
Sie brauchen eine gute Ausbildung.	You need a good education.	gehe ich zur Musikgruppe	I have been going to a music group
		Ich besuche einen (Computer-)Kurs.	I attend a (computer) course.
		Ich habe einen (Textverarbeitungs-)Kurs besucht.	I attended a (word-processing) course.

Had a look ☐ Nearly there ☐ Nailed it ☐

Ein Hochschulabschluss / Arbeitserfahrung ist nicht notwendig.	A degree / Work experience is not necessary.		
Wenn Sie einen Hochschulabschluss machen, verdienen Sie schneller ein höheres Gehalt.	If you graduate, you earn a higher salary more quickly.	Ich bekomme gute Noten.	I get good grades.
		Meine Noten sind nicht so gut.	My grades are not so good.
Ihr Gehalt ist niedrig / großzügig / ausgezeichnet.	Your salary is low / generous / excellent.	Meine Durchschnittsnote ist …	My average grade is …
Die Arbeitsbedingungen sind besonders gut / schlecht.	The working conditions are particularly good / bad.	Ich habe einen Teilzeitjob als (Touristenführer(in)).	I have a part-time job as a (tour guide).
Es gibt gute / wenige Aufstiegsmöglichkeiten.	There are good / few opportunities for promotion.	Letzten Sommer habe ich als (Freiwillige(r)) gearbeitet.	Last summer I worked as a (volunteer).
		Ich bin …	I am …
		kreativ	creative

Had a look ☐ Nearly there ☐ Nailed it ☐

K 7

Sie arbeiten …	You work …	musikalisch	musical
auf Baustellen	on building sites	geduldig	patient
bei einer Firma	for a company	fleißig	hard-working
freiberuflich von zu Hause aus	freelance from home	pünktlich	punctual

Had a look ☐ Nearly there ☐ Nailed it ☐

in einem Geschäft	in a shop
in einem Altenheim	in a care home for older people
in einem Krankenhaus	in a hospital
zuerst	first(ly)
danach	after that
dann	then
anschließend	finally

Mein Lebenslauf — My CV

die Schulbildung	school education
der Schulabschluss	school-leaving qualification
die Schulleistung	school achievement
die freiwillige Arbeit	voluntary work
der Hochschulabschluss	degree
die Berufserfahrung	professional experience
die Freizeitaktivitäten	leisure activities

Had a look ☐ Nearly there ☐ Nailed it ☐

Bewerbungen — Applications

Ich interessiere mich für den Job als …, weil …	I'm interested in the job as … because …
ich (in Mathe) begabt bin	I'm good at / gifted in (maths)
ich (in der Touristik) arbeiten möchte	I would like to work in (tourism)
ich verantwortungsbewusst bin	I'm responsible
ich selbstständig sein will	I want to be independent
Seit drei Jahren … bin ich Mitglied im Orchester	For three years … I have been a member of an orchestra
bin ich Kapitän der (Handball-)Mannschaft	I have been captain of the (handball) team

Traumberufe — Dream jobs

Als Kind wollte ich (Clown / Feuerwehrmann) werden.	As a child, I wanted to be a (clown / firefighter).
Ich möchte … arbeiten. als (Manager(in))	I would like to work … as a (manager)
im Ausland	abroad
in (den USA)	in (the USA)
freiwillig	voluntarily
in einem Elefantenheim	in an elephant home / elephant sanctuary
bei der Europäischen Kommission	for the European Commission

bei einer (internationalen) Firma	for an (international) company
beim Zirkus	for a circus
Ich würde gern …	I would like …
in einer Hütte in den Alpen wohnen	to live in a hut / a cabin in the Alps
nach (Thailand) reisen	to travel to (Thailand)
ein Jahr in (Thailand) verbringen	to spend a year in (Thailand)
eine Lehre machen	to do an apprenticeship
Marketing machen	to do marketing

Had a look ☐ **Nearly there** ☐ **Nailed it** ☐

Sprachen öffnen Türen
Languages open doors

Im Moment lerne ich (Spanisch), um …	At the moment I'm learning (Spanish) in order to …
mich um einen guten Job zu bewerben	apply for a good job
die Leute / die Kultur / die Landessprache besser kennenzulernen	get to know the people / the culture / the national language better
nach (Spanien) auszuwandern	emigrate to (Spain)
Ich lerne (Deutsch), um …	I'm learning (German) in order to …
(an der Börse) zu arbeiten	work (at the stock exchange)
meine (Deutsch-)Kenntnisse zu verbessern	improve my knowledge (of German)
(die Liedertexte / Opern) richtig zu verstehen	understand (the lyrics / operas) properly
Ich möchte (Griechisch) lernen, um …	I would like to learn (Greek) in order to …
durch das Land zu reisen	travel around the country
mit Leuten in ihrer Muttersprache zu kommunizieren	communicate with people in their native language
mich zu amüsieren	have fun
Im Moment lerne ich (Mandarin), weil es … ist.	At the moment I'm learning (Mandarin) because it's …
ein Pflichtfach	a compulsory subject
nötig	necessary, essential
mir wichtig	important to me

Had a look ☐ **Nearly there** ☐ **Nailed it** ☐

Kapitel 7 Wörter

Extra words I should know for reading and listening activities

Berufe	*Jobs*
der/die Angestellte	employee
der/die Arbeitgeber(in)	employer
der/die Bauarbeiter(in)*	builder
der/die Bauer/Bäuerin*	farmer
der/die Ingenieur(in)	engineer
der/die Kassierer(in)	cashier
der/die Kollege/Kollegin	colleague
der/die Sprachassistent(in)	language assistant
der/die Sprachliebhaber(in)	language lover
der/die Touristenführer(in)	tourist guide
der/die Vertreter(in)	representative, sales rep

ausgebildet	*qualified*
beilegen	*to enclose, to attach*
benötigen	*to need*
erfahren	*experienced*
sich konzentrieren	*to concentrate*
sich vorstellen	*to introduce oneself*
absolvieren	*to complete (course), to pass (exam)*
Jura	*law (subject)*
Medizin	*medicine (subject)*
das Semester(-)	*semester*
abwechslungsreich	*varied*
lehrreich	*educational*
das Familienleben	*family life*
der Lebensstil	*lifestyle*

Had a look ☐ **Nearly there** ☐ **Nailed it** ☐   **Had a look** ☐ **Nearly there** ☐ **Nailed it** ☐

Bei der Arbeit	*At work*
der Arbeitsplatz (-plätze)	workplace
die Besprechung(en)	meeting
die Gesellschaft(en)	company, society
die Kinderkrippe(n)	crèche
die Klinik(en)	clinic
die Konferenz(en)	conference
die Nachhilfe	private tuition
die Schichtarbeit	shift work
die Stelle(n)	job
der Termin(e)	appointment
die Touristik	tourism
das Treffen(-)	meeting

Had a look ☐ **Nearly there** ☐ **Nailed it** ☐

Bewerbungen	*Applications*
die Anzeige(n)	advertisement
der Bewerbungsbrief(e)	letter of application
das Bewerbungsformular(e)	application form
der Ehrgeiz	ambition
der Eindruck (Eindrücke)	impression
die Fähigkeit(en)	skill, ability
der Lohn	wage
die Möglichkeit(en)	possibility
die Notwendigkeit(en)	necessity
der Rat	advice
das Stellenangebot(e)	job offer, situations vacant
das Vorstellungsgespräch(e)	interview
die Zukunftspläne (pl)	plans for the future

Had a look ☐ **Nearly there** ☐ **Nailed it** ☐

> *Look out for word families when working out the meaning of words, but remember to use the context of the text to help you too.
>
> *Bauen* means 'to build' and *anbauen* means 'to grow' and you have come across several words using the stem *bau*:
>
> *Der Bauer* and *der Bauarbeiter* both look similar, but one means 'farmer' and the other 'builder'.
>
> *Der Bauernhof* and *die Baustelle* also look quite similar, but which is a 'farm', and which a 'building site'?
>
> Using the language around the words will help you work out the meaning:
>
> *Ich wohne auf einem Bauernhof auf dem Land.*
> I live on a farm in the countryside.
>
> Here, the verb *wohne* and the location *auf dem Land* help you decide that *Bauernhof* must be a farm rather than a building site.

Kapitel 8 Wörter

Words I should know for speaking and writing activities

Festivals und Events	**Festivals and events**
Letzten Sommer / Mai …	Last summer / May …
Letztes Jahr / Wochenende …	Last year / weekend …
habe ich das (Festival) gesehen	I saw the (festival)
bin ich zum (Event) gefahren	I went to the (event)
Ich habe dort …	I … there.
Fußball / Saxofon gespielt	played football / saxophone
nette Leute kennengelernt	met nice people
die Sehenswürdigkeiten besichtigt	visited the sights
die Spiele / die Bands gesehen	saw the games / bands
Das Konzert / Turnier hat in … stattgefunden.	The concert / tournament took place in …
Deutschland / England / Australien	Germany / England / Australia
Ich bin im Meer geschwommen.	I swam in the sea.
Das Festival war / fand ich …	The festival was / I found the festival …
etwas langweilig	a bit boring
sehr lustig	very funny
total spannend / super / toll	totally exciting / super / great
ziemlich laut	quite loud

Had a look ☐ Nearly there ☐ Nailed it ☐

Ein sportliches Event	**A sporting event**
der Streckenposten(–)	checkpoint
der Informationskiosk(e)	information stand
der Führungswagen(–)	lead car
die Ziellinie(n)	finish line
das Souvenirgeschäft(e)	souvenir shop
der Massageraum (–räume)	massage room
die Kleiderabgabe	cloakroom
die Kinderkrippe(n)	crèche

Had a look ☐ Nearly there ☐ Nailed it ☐

Die Olympischen Winterspiele	**The Winter Olympics**
(1976) fanden die Olympischen Spiele in (Innsbruck) statt.	(In 1976) the Olympic Games took place in (Innsbruck).
(1.200) Sportler aus (37) Ländern haben teilgenommen.	(1,200) sportspeople from (37) countries took part.
Es gab Wettbewerbe in (6) Sportarten.	There were competitions in (6) sports.
Ein Vorteil ist / war …	An advantage is / was …
Ein Nachteil ist / war …	A disadvantage is / was …
die Baustelle(n)	building site / construction site
die Gastgeberstadt (–städte)	host city
die Lärmbelastung	noise pollution
die Luftverschmutzung	air pollution
der Stau(s)	traffic jam
der Tourist(en)	tourist
der Zeitdruck	time pressure

Had a look ☐ Nearly there ☐ Nailed it ☐

Gesellschaftliche Probleme	**Social problems**
der Alkoholiker	alcoholic (person)
stinken	to stink
vapen	to vape
der Lungenkrebs	lung cancer
aufgeben	to give up
betrunken	drunk
süchtig	addicted
illegal	illegal
die E-Zigarette(n)	e-cigarette
der Gruppendruck	peer pressure
ausprobieren	to try
unsozial	anti-social
etwas Neues	something new
nichts Positives	nothing positive
viel Negatives	a lot that is negative
alles Mögliche	everything possible
wenig Bewundernswertes	little to admire

Had a look ☐ Nearly there ☐ Nailed it ☐

Meiner Meinung nach …	In my opinion …
trinkt man Alkohol, weil das cool ist	people drink alcohol because it's cool
raucht man, weil das entspannend ist	people smoke because it's relaxing
nimmt man Drogen, weil man unter Gruppendruck steht	people take drugs because of peer pressure
Ich finde, …	I find …
Alkohol ist eine Geldverschwendung	alcohol is a waste of money
Rauchen ist teuer	smoking is expensive
Drogen sind schrecklich	drugs are terrible
Man sollte Alkohol vermeiden, weil das gefährlich ist.	You ought to avoid alcohol because (drinking alcohol) is dangerous.

43

Kapitel 8 Wörter

Man sollte Rauchen vermeiden, weil das ekelhaft ist.	You ought to avoid smoking because it's disgusting.
Man sollte Drogen vermeiden, weil das tödlich ist.	You ought to avoid drugs because (taking drugs) is lethal.
Ich werde in Zukunft aufgeben.	I will give up in future.
Ich würde das Risiko nie eingehen.	I would never take the risk.
Einerseits …	On the one hand …
Andererseits …	On the other hand …
Ich stimme da nicht zu.	I don't agree.
Vielleicht …, aber …	Perhaps … but …

Had a look ☐ **Nearly there** ☐ **Nailed it** ☐

Die Länder / Countries

Bulgarien	Bulgaria
Deutschland	Germany
Finnland	Finland
Griechenland	Greece
Großbritannien	Great Britain
Italien	Italy
Kanada	Canada
Kroatien	Croatia
Lettland	Latvia
Litauen	Lithuania
die Niederlande	the Netherlands
Norwegen	Norway
Portugal	Portugal
Rumänien	Romania
Schweden	Sweden
Tschechien	Czech Republic
Ungarn	Hungary
Zypern	Cyprus

Had a look ☐ **Nearly there** ☐ **Nailed it** ☐

Die Armut / Poverty

das Interessante	the interesting thing
das Gute	the good thing
die Minderheit(en)	minority
die Mehrheit(en)	majority
von Armut betroffen	affected by poverty
von Armut bedroht	threatened by poverty
die Ursache(n)	cause
die Arbeitslosigkeit	unemployment
der geringe Lohn	low wage / pay
die Schuld(en)	debt
der Bildungsmangel	lack of education
der Immigrant(e) / die Immigrantin(nen)	immigrant
die Arbeitsstelle(n)	job

Had a look ☐ **Nearly there** ☐ **Nailed it** ☐

der/die Obdachlose(n)	homeless person
die Nacht auf der Straße verbringen	to spend the night on the streets
im Wohnheim schlafen	to sleep in a hostel
bei Freunden schlafen	to sleep at friends' houses
die medizinische Versorgung	medical care
von zu Hause weglaufen	to run away from home
die Arbeit verlieren	to lose your job
die Gewalt	violence
gewalttätig	violent
die Misshandlung	ill-treatment, cruelty
der (sexuelle) Missbrauch	(sexual) abuse
das Straßenkind(er)	street child

Had a look ☐ **Nearly there** ☐ **Nailed it** ☐

Umwelt macht Schule / Setting environmental standards at school

Man könnte / sollte / würde …	We could / should / would …
den Müll trennen	sort the rubbish
Biomüll kompostieren	compost organic waste
eine Solaranlage installieren	install solar panels
Bienenvölker im Schulgarten halten	keep bee-hives in the school garden
Druckerpatronen / Kopierkartuschen recyceln	recycle printer / copier cartridges
Nistkästen für Vögel bauen	build bird boxes
eine Fahrradwoche organisieren	organise a bike week
Energie sparen	save energy
das Licht ausschalten	turn the light off
die Natur schützen (Naturschutz) ist wichtiger als (Müll zu trennen).	protect nature (Protecting nature) is more important than (sorting rubbish).
Der Müll ist das wichtigste Problem.	Rubbish is the most important problem.
Man sollte weniger Auto fahren.	We should drive less.
Man könnte öfter den Müll trennen.	We could sort the rubbish more often.

Had a look ☐ **Nearly there** ☐ **Nailed it** ☐

Wie werden wir „grüner"? / How do we become 'greener'?

| das Aussterben von Tierarten | the extinction of animal species |
| die Abholzung | deforestation |

Kapitel 8 Wörter

die globale Erwärmung	global warming
die Lärmbelastung	noise pollution
die Luftverschmutzung	air pollution
die Überbevölkerung	over-population
die Überschwemmungen	flooding
die Wüstenbildung	desertification
… ist sehr alarmierend / gefährlich / traurig, weil …	… is very alarming / dangerous / sad because …
… ist das wichtigste / größte Problem, weil …	… is the most important / biggest problem because …
man krank werden kann	people can become ill
so viele Menschen an Hungersnot leiden	so many people suffer from starvation
sie das Leben / die Infrastruktur bedrohen	they threaten life / the infrastructure
das Ozonloch größer wird	the hole in the ozone layer gets bigger
der Planet nicht unendlich viele Menschen ernähren kann	the planet cannot feed unlimited numbers of people
wir in Zukunft diese Tiere nie mehr sehen werden	we won't see these animals any more in the future
die Wälder weniger Kohlendioxid aus der Luft absorbieren	the forests absorb less carbon dioxide from the air
der saure Regen die Meere vergiftet	acid rain poisons the oceans
die Gletscher schmelzen	the glaciers melt
der Meeresspiegel steigt	the sea level rises

Had a look ☐ Nearly there ☐ Nailed it ☐

Wenn man …	If we …
die Luftverschmutzung reduzieren will	want to reduce air pollution
weniger Öl / Kohle / Gas nutzen will	want to use less oil / coal / gas
das Kohlendioxid in der Luft reduzieren will	want to reduce carbon dioxide in the air
keine Atomkraftwerke bauen will	don't want to build nuclear power stations
die Meere nicht vergiften will	don't want to poison the oceans
Tierarten nicht verlieren will	don't want to lose animal species
… sollte / könnte man …	… we should / could …
in erneuerbare Energien / Windenergie / Sonnenenergie investieren	invest in renewable energies / wind energy / solar energy
öfter mit dem Rad / öffentlichen Verkehrsmitteln fahren	travel more often by bike / public transport
weniger Ölkatastrophen verursachen	cause fewer oil spills
die Natur schützen	protect nature
Windkraftanlagen / Solarkraftwerke / Wasserkraftwerke bauen	build wind power stations / solar power stations / hydroelectric power stations
effektiver Energie und Geld sparen	save energy and money more effectively
die Wälder nicht zerstören	not destroy the forests

Had a look ☐ Nearly there ☐ Nailed it ☐

Kampagnen und gute Zwecke
Campaigns and good causes

Bali	Bali
Costa Rica	Costa Rica
die Malediven	the Maldives
Namibia	Namibia
Nepal	Nepal
arm	poor
blind	blind
erfolgreich	successful
Du könntest … arbeiten.	You could work …
ehrenamtlich / freiwillig	voluntarily
bei einer Tierschutzorganisation	for an animal protection organisation
bei einer Umweltschutzorganisation	for an environmental organisation
bei einer Hilfsorganisation	for an aid organisation
mit armen / blinden Kindern	with poor / blind children
mit Straßenkindern	with street children
mit wilden Tieren	with wild animals

Had a look ☐ Nearly there ☐ Nailed it ☐

K 8

Kapitel 8 Wörter

Extra words I should know for reading and listening activities

Ein sportliches Event — A sporting event
das Turnier(e)	tournament
die Endrunde	finals
das Halbfinale(–)	semi-final
kämpfen	to fight
das Energiegetränk(e)	energy drink
der Kleiderbeutel(–)	bag of clothes
der/die Läufer(in)	runner
das Massagebett(en)	massage bed
der/die Physiotherapeut(in)	physiotherapist
das Turnen	gymnastics

Had a look ☐ Nearly there ☐ Nailed it ☐

Festivals und Events — Festivals and events
aus aller Welt	from all over the world
das Drehbuch(–bücher)	(film) script
der/die Einwohner(in)	inhabitant
die Kapazität(en)	capacity
der/die Komponist(in)	composer
die Modenschau(en)*	fashion show
der/die Regisseur(in)	director (film)
begrüßen	to greet, to welcome

Had a look ☐ Nearly there ☐ Nailed it ☐

Gesellschaftliche Probleme — Social problems
der/die Drogenhändler(in)	drug dealer
der/die Drogensüchtige(n)	drug addict
das Medikament(e)	medicine
die Spirituosen (pl)	spirits (alcohol)
die Spritze(n)	syringe, injection
die Sucht (Süchte)	addiction
der Verbrennungsprodukt(e)	combustion product
abhängig sein von	to be dependent on
Nikotin enthalten	to contain nicotine
Leben retten	to save lives
in der Öffentlichkeit	in public
die Ader(–)	vein
das Blut	blood
das Herz	heart
der Herzanfall(–anfälle)	heart attack
die Leber	liver
der Magen	stomach
atmen	to breathe
das Bewusstsein	consciousness
bewusstlos	unconscious

Had a look ☐ Nearly there ☐ Nailed it ☐

Die Armut — Poverty
der/die Bedürftige	somebody in need
die Eingliederung	integration
die Ernährung	food, nourishment
die Gleichheit	equality
das Heim(e)	home, care home
die Isomatte(n)	camping mat, sleeping pad
der Schlafsack(–säcke)	sleeping bag
die Sorge(n)	worry
den Kontakt abbrechen	to break off contact
benachteiligen	to disadvantage
sorgen für	to care for
hilflos	helpless
menschlich	human, humane

Had a look ☐ Nearly there ☐ Nailed it ☐

Die Umwelt — The environment
der Dschungel(–)	jungle
das Erdbeben(–)	earthquake
die Naturschätze (pl)	natural resources
der Orkan(e)	hurricane
der Regenwald(–wälder)	rainforest
das Salzwasser	salt water
der Vulkan(e)	volcano
der Mangel an	lack of
drohen, bedrohen	to threaten
fehlen	to lack
retten	to save
sterben	to die
überleben	to survive
vergiften	to contaminate
verschmutzen	to pollute

Had a look ☐ Nearly there ☐ Nailed it ☐

Wie werden wir „grüner"? — How do we become 'greener'?
die Atomenergie	nuclear energy
der Biokraftstoff(e)*	organic fuel
die Energiesparmethode(n)	means of saving energy
der Ökostrom	'green' electricity
der Karton(s)	cardboard, cardboard box
der Verpackungsmüll	packaging waste
die Regierung(en)	government
der/die Umweltsprecher(in)	environmental spokesperson
schmutzig	dirty
verändern	to change
verbrauchen	to use, to consume (energy)

Had a look ☐ Nearly there ☐ Nailed it ☐

K8

46

Kapitel 8 Wörter

Kampagnen und gute Zwecke / *Campaigns and good causes*

die Armut	poverty
der faire Handel	fair trade
die Hungersnot(-nöte)	famine
das Kinderheim(e)	children's home
der Krieg(e)	war
das Menschenrecht(e)*	human right
die Tankstelle(n)	petrol station
das Trinkwasser	drinking water
die Wellblechhütte(n)	corrugated-iron hut
der Wohltätigkeitsverein(e)	charity
bedürftig	needy
unglücklich	unfortunate
sich lohnen	to be worthwhile, to be worth it

Had a look ☐ **Nearly there** ☐ **Nailed it** ☐

---

*Use your knowledge of German to work out the meaning of compound nouns. These longer words are usually made up of several smaller words, and you will often be able to work out their meaning by breaking them down and then putting the meanings back together again:

die Modenschau → *Mode* (fashion) + *Schau* (show) = fashion show

das Menschenrecht → *Mensch* (person / human) + *Recht* (right) = human right

Sometimes you will need to take the sense of the German word and think a bit more broadly to come up with the correct English translation:

der Biokraftstoff → *Bio* (organic) + *Kraft* (power) + *Stoff* (substance) = 'organic fuel' rather than 'organic power substance'

ISBN 978-1-292-1324-02